A PLACE WHERE
NEEDS & ROSES
GROW

Joan Spencer

 **Windshift Press**

Library and Archives Canada Cataloguing in Publication
Spencer, Joan, 1966-
A place where weeds and roses grow / Joan Spencer.

ISBN 0-9736560-8-5
1. Compulsive gambling. 2. Compulsive gamblers--Canada--Biography.
I. Title.

RC569.5.G35S64 2006   616.85'8410092   C2006-900535-4

Publisher/Distributor
Windshift Press
P O Box 1176
Ladysmith,
BC, Canada, V9G 1A8
E-mail: press@windshift.bc.ca

Cover Design: madebydesign
Layout: Beachwalker Studio

PRINTED IN CANADA

For my Family
and
For God

Thank you for loving me
when I was most unlovable

MY HEART GOES OUT to all those who are suffering with the agonizing addiction of compulsive gambling, as well as those affected by the affliction of a loved one. My heart knows only too well your pain, your sorrow, your shame. I hope my story inspires within you a desire to seek help for your own addiction, or to support your loved one in doing so.

This is a true story describing actual events. The names of all persons herein have been altered in an attempt to protect their privacy. Any person's name or any situation contained herein resembling that of an actual person (other than that intended by me, the author, of course) is purely coincidental.

Furthermore, please be advised that the contents of this story is of a graphic nature and may be disturbing to some readers. I hold nothing back. There is simply no way to sugarcoat the bitter truth about my compulsive gambling addiction.

My story begins with some mostly happy pieces of my childhood, followed by some not-always-so-happy pieces of my teenage years. I continue on to reveal more pieces of myself, both good and bad, segments of my life which I consider to be "pivotal events;" a variety of experiences which may or may not have contributed in some measure to my becoming a compulsive gambling addict. Judge things for yourself. In essence, I lay bare my soul for you on the pages of this book. I do so in order to expose the raw, honest makings of a compulsive gambling addict. What makes "IT" tick? As I said, you be the judge.

So go ahead now. Read my story.
And by all means, be horrified.
I expect nothing less...

A PLACE WHERE
WEEDS & ROSES
GROW

MY AGONIZING ADDICTION to compulsive gambling was for me, a near-death experience. Not your typical near-death experience lasting a mere few minutes complete with a pretty white light and long-lost loved ones extending welcoming hands to join them in the glorious afterlife. No, mine was not at all like that. First of all, it lasted for nearly six years. And there was no "white light." There was, however, a red light and it flashed like crazy whenever I won something. It sat atop the slot machine. Reminded me of an exquisite red rose when it lit up like that. Didn't take long, however, for me to prick my finger on one of its thorns...

As I stood gazing at the crimson bead forming there at my fingertip, I felt something slither around my ankle. Before I had a chance to react the weed had wound its way up to my thigh. As it slipped around my waist, I began to scream... But no sound emerged. The weed was at my throat, its cold, sinewy fingers suffocating my pleas for help.

Before I knew it, I was surrounded in darkness. *Am I dead?* I wondered. Turned out I wasn't, but it wouldn't be long before I found myself wishing I were.

My soul's fateful journey into the dark world of compulsive gambling began in 1994. My physical body stayed behind to be a wonderful wife and devoted daughter, a sweet sister and faithful friend, and wretch...

1

A Blissful Family of Five

I grew up in a small town called Kimberley—an exciting and fun tourist trap set at the foot of the Rocky Mountains in beautiful British Columbia. There, I was blessed with a happy childhood, nourished by two loving parents who provided well for me emotionally, spiritually and materially.

Kamloops, BC was my actual place of birth, and as my first cries rang out, tears flowed also from the eyes of the woman who had just given birth to me. They were *not* tears of joy. The young woman was devastated, her heart broken. My mother was not ready for me; she was not prepared emotionally or financially to care for a child. Her baby girl would have to become someone else's bundle of joy...

George and Rita were a happy couple with just three, small things missing from their marriage. Unable to conceive children of their own, their hearts ached with longing for three little ones to complete their family. They adopted their first child, James Mark, in 1965. The selfless act of my birth mother giving me, Joan Marie, up for adoption in 1966 filled the second void in George and Rita's life. My sister, Amy Jo, completed our blissful family of five in 1969.

Dad created fond nicknames for each member of our family; he became "Father Bear," my mother "Mother Hen," my brother "Beanstalk" and my sister "Charlie." I was known simply as "Chick."

It wouldn't take long for my mother to discover that her new bundle of joy named Joan was a tad more than she'd bargained for. Lurking just beneath the innocent facade of twinkling eyes and rosy cheeks was a most mischievous personality. Naughty as naughty could be, that was me, stubbornly defying the word "no" at every given opportunity.

Before my dimpled legs could carry me, I roamed the house in my wheeled walker. Around and around and around I went, with tiny fingers in search of everything forbidden. The more my mother protested, the more bound and determined I became. Planting her hands firmly at her hips, she held her ground, sternly refusing me access to the drawer of her sewing machine table (which, of course, contained scissors, needles, and so forth). It quickly grew into an obsession; I had to discover what secret treasures lay inside the heavily guarded drawer. Securely tying it shut merely increased my curiosity, fine-tuning the dexterity of my chubby, little fingers.

Every minute of every day became an exhausting challenge of my mother's patience. Ten grueling years she spent at home with her trying terrors before re-entering the workforce, which was nothing short of heroic in my book (although, perhaps, an ideal case study for one of Dr. Phil's psychology books...).

My mother was a kind and gentle soul, suited perfectly for her role as a Registered Nurse. She went about the community providing home care, tending to the sick with love and compassion. As well, a day did not pass without our family being thoroughly tended to. Mother crawled out of bed at the crack of dawn to get it all started. Five days a week, she thoughtfully prepared bagged lunches for us kids to take to school. Now these were not just any old lunches stuffed into brown paper bags; each and every one was carefully crafted with something nutritious to counteract our favorite sweet treat. My father's lunch was of special design, consisting of small Tupperware containers filled with fruit salad, peanuts, pickles and pepperoni, cheese and crackers, and homemade cookies. A favorite chocolate bar also made its way into the mix, accompanied by a steaming hot thermos of soup. The assortment of goodies was packed neatly into a large, gray lunch-pail that must have weighed five pounds.

Every Sunday, our family gathered for a delicious roast beef dinner, complete with Yorkshire Puddings and gravy. This was a traditional English favorite of my father's. My mother spent almost every waking moment caring for her family. Her nickname, "Mother Hen," "Hen" for short, could not have been more fitting.

Growing up, not once did I witness my mother lose her temper. Not to any significant degree anyway. I could not help but laugh at her occasional mild outburst, where her face would redden and she'd loudly exclaim: "Oh good gravy!" or "Heavens to Betsy!" or "Honest to Peter!" That was as close to cursing as my mother ever came. I suppose it's safe to assume Betsy and Peter were the makers of the good gravy she raved about... Considering the fact that at least two of her three children were hellions, I must say, Mom's restraint in using such gentle expletives was nothing short of miraculous.

I'm sure my mother remembers well the day my brother and I

disappeared without a trace. It happened the precise moment in which she turned her back to bathe our younger sister. My big brother was six at the time, and I, barely four.

Panic overwhelmed her as she searched high and low, her shrill voice echoing the hallways as she desperately searched the house. Mother Hen raced outside, growing more and more anxious by the minute. Around the outside of the house she ran, fretting and desperately scouring the yard for her precious chicks. But we were nowhere to be found.

Hysteria was on the verge of attack when Mercy intervened; my mother spotted two filthy kids strolling up the road towards the house. Seeing the angry expression on her face as we neared the yard, I promptly stuffed my new pet snake into my pants' pocket.

Mom scolded us relentlessly, clucking on and on as she corralled her mischievous chicks into the house. Mother Hen's feathers were further ruffled moments later when she discovered that beneath all the mud and dirt caked on my clothing—Heavens to Betsy!—I had peed my pants!

My mother plopped me down on the small, wooden table in the laundry room and began removing my soiled clothing. Slowly, she peeled my soggy pants down, squatting on her haunches as she did so, all the while chastising her small, grinning girl. Obviously, there was only one way to atone for my bad behavior... Hopping down from the table, I grabbed hold of my urine-soaked pants to reach into the front, left pocket. Without further ado, I extracted my hand to thrust the dangling peace offering towards my mother. Bewilderment struck when I received neither pardon nor praise, but a bloodcurdling scream! Promptly, my brother was instructed to remove the wretched demon snake from my tightly clenched fist and dispose of it in the trashcan outside.

I was absolutely horrified by my mother's heartless betrayal. The moment she finished fussing over me, I raced outside to rescue my friend from the garbage can. I was relieved to discover that he'd slept peacefully through the entire ordeal. Of course, I'd had no idea whatsoever that Snuggles, my sleepy serpent, was as dead as a doornail—likely the result of a little too much asphyxiation, administered as I so lovingly carried him home.

Into a little dickens I grew, a tomboy from head to toe. I never bothered with boring Barbie dolls and the like; instead I collected frogs, turtles, snakes and salamanders and—of course—a variety of tasty night crawlers to feed my captive crew. Our back yard was likely the only one in the neighborhood adorned with an old cast iron bathtub. It served well as a miniature pond for my collection of swamp dwelling creatures, although few of them survived long enough to boast to their friends.

Encouraged by my father's example, my love for animals grew larger with each passing day. I never missed an opportunity to accompany my dad when visiting "The People with the Dog." Admittedly, the memory includes not the slightest trace of either the man or his wife, but my mind reminisces most vividly of every delightful detail of their black and white Boston Terrier. Oh, how I loved that dog! On each visit, my bestest buddy, Tiny, and I would spend a good hour playing ball. Over and over and over, I would throw the ball the length of the yard, until finally the poor pooch would nearly drop dead from exhaustion. Tiny would appear near rabid with that bubbling white froth at his mouth, his flanks heaving in and out, and his thick, pink tongue lolling over the side of his teeth like a slab of sweaty ham. It would take the poor fellow an entire week to recuperate from the crippling event. No one had had the heart to hinder my happiness, and I was unaware that the little guy was pushing thirteen and ridden with arthritis.

Finally, my father devised a secret plan to save both a little, old dog from keeling over and a beloved daughter from a whole lot of heartache...

Happy to be in the company of my father, although not overly excited with the trip's itinerary, I sat in silence en route to the airport to help him pick up a package of school supplies. Upon arrival I stood beside my father, my small hand embedded within his large one, as we waited patiently for the conveyor belt to bring the expected parcel. My eyes lit up when I spotted a cage containing a black and white puppy riding amid the various items.

"Oh, look, Dad! It's a Boston Terrier!" I exclaimed excitedly, jumping up and down.

"Why don't you go over and take a look at the tag on the cage. See who it belongs to," Dad suggested casually.

Like a seasoned sprinter, I raced over to take a peek. "Dad, Dad!" I shouted at the top of my lungs. "It has our Spencer name on it!"

Happiness danced in my father's eyes as he walked over and stood next to me. Peering down into my overjoyed face, he said, "Perhaps we should take the little fellow home with us."

I sat in the back seat on the ride home, chattering away at my new best friend. Excitedly, I told him of all the fun things we were going to do together. Deciding we should get to it, Puppy grabbed hold of my sleeve and began a game of tug-of-war. I named him Tug right then and there.

Tug needed something to ride around in. I decided on a cardboard box when we got home. All that was required was a rope to fasten through the existing handle, and a makeshift window for my pal to peek through. Of course, the largest, sharpest knife would be required for such a project...

I poked the knife tip through the side of the box and pressed downward. It wouldn't budge. Standing on tiptoes, I strategically planted my left hand on the table at the base of the box and began sawing the blade back and forth with my right. I then leaned down on the knife, pushing with all my might. The knife gave way immediately, slicing through the cardboard as if it were warm chocolate.

It took me a moment to realize that my thumb was nearly lopped off. The incision was made so rapidly that I'd barely felt the knife penetrate my flesh, the cut so clean that it did not bleed right away. This, of course, was anything but a bad thing, as it allowed me to pull apart my flesh and gawk in wonder at the severed tendon.

Mom entered the kitchen and asked me what I was doing.

"Look!" I said, proudly displaying for her my gaping wound.

"Good gravy!" she shrieked, grabbing hold of my thumb and binding it together with a dishtowel. She nearly dislocated my shoulder as she yanked me out to the car.

Two hours of surgery later I lay in the hospital cot, anxiously awaiting visitors to sign my cast. My grade five classmates were entirely enthralled with my explicit account of the event (worthy, no doubt, of appearing in the next Stephen King novel). A wee bit of embellishment came into play to achieve the desired effect, I admit, but only a bit:

'The gigantic, super-sharp butcher-knife sliced right through my thumb like it was a chunk of chicken, and then it just hanged off my hand by a skinny piece of skin. It was really cool! Veins popped out all over the place and blood gushed out like in the horror movies. I got really dizzy and blind by all the blood that got in my eyes, but somehow I found my mom. Then I fainted. Not because I was scared or anything, but because almost all my blood fell out. My Mom rescued me just before I died. Good thing she's a nurse. It took twenty whole doctors to sew my thumb back on. They told me I am a very brave survivor. The end.'

My father was a well-respected member of the community. He was the school principal and a teacher of mathematics, demonstrating strong ethics and a genuine passion for educating his students.

Being head of our household, and a fairly strict disciplinarian, Dad expected proper behavior from his three children, along with reasonable school grades, of course. Although he wore the pants in our family, he often slackened that tight belt of authority long enough to join us in some frivolous activities. I remember as a little girl, giggling until my stomach ached as I watched my father pirouette gracefully about the room like a ballerina while belting out a verse of, "I've got a lovely bunch of coconuts! There they are all standing in a row!"

Dad and I would get so carried away with our wit competitions that my little sister would moan and groan and accuse us of being "sick." One day, as our family sat around the dinner table, Dad picked up the milk carton to pass it slowly back and forth, back and forth before my eyes, and then exclaimed, "Now this milk is pasteurized!" I repeated this pun often, milking it for all it was worth.

I fondly recall the event that finally inspired my father to re-christen his favorite child, "Chick." At the school he reigned over as Principal, a classroom science project was underway that featured an incubator filled with shiny, white chicken eggs. A room full of young students could barely contain their excitement as they awaited the great hatching event to unfold. An untimely power failure, however, would leave them sadly disappointed. I, on the other hand, was utterly ecstatic when my father arrived home with the small den of delight.

I kept a watchful eye over my delicately shelled brood, and marveled at the miracle of their birth. I giggled joyfully as tiny chicks pecked their way into the world, gazed in awe at their damp, wriggling bodies and longed to hold them in my hands.

The threat of having my newfound friends torn away from me was more than I could bear, so my father allowed them to remain in my care a little longer than originally planned. He made it perfectly clear, however, that they could not stay indefinitely, as mother would never approve of having full-grown chickens clucking around the house. Sheesh! You'd think a "Mother Hen" would have a wee bit of compassion...

They soon became a boisterous bunch of fuzzy, yellow, peeping chicks, and I loved them all. So, too, came the heart-wrenching day when I was forced to tell them goodbye. Father assured me that the school children would love them as much as I, but secretly, I had my doubts. Just to be sure,

I checked in on them from time to time at their new home. Until I became entirely preoccupied with my new pet hamster, that is.

Poor, plump Lullaby got out of his cage one day for an adventurous game of hide-and-go-seek. I sincerely hope he enjoyed his brief encounter with freedom. After searching high and low and to and fro, I finally spotted Lullaby on the floor of the closet, just as he ran behind the case containing my sewing machine. I stooped over to lift the heavy object with the intention of relocating it to the corner, but just as I lowered it back down, Lullaby scurried underneath. I cringed as I heard the crunch. As quickly as I could, I raised the case back up. But it was much too late. My fuzzy friend was hopping around like a defective wind-up toy with blood spurting out in every direction.

Scooping up the tiny ball of twitching fur I raced upstairs, yelling hysterically for my mother. If anyone could save him, it was she... She was a nurse!

Mom cried as hard as I did as I placed the lifeless body of my beloved hamster in the makeshift coffin lined with Kleenex. A Popsicle-stick cross jutting out from a mound of dirt in our backyard was all that remained of my sweet, little Lullaby.

My childhood faith was a simple one, like most, I would imagine, pure and clean and uncluttered by all the grown-up stuff kids have yet to accumulate. In my young mind, God was a very big, magic "guy" who lived somewhere up in the sky. He was nice and gentle and a very, very good listener. I remember praying the words, *Now I lay me down to sleep ... I pray the Lord my soul to keep... If I should die before I wake... I pray the Lord my soul to take.* And I remember praying many meaningful prayers of my very own... *Please God, I'd really like a new puppy... Please God, I'd really like a new kitty-cat... Please God, let Lullaby into Heaven...*

Every Sunday, our family would attend Mass at Sacred Heart Church, a simple structure made fancy with stained glass windows, which sat atop a hill where it kept watch over our little town. As a youngster, I don't remember a whole lot about the service, other than wishing I had a pillow to put between my bony behind and the cold, hard pew ... that and being shushed by my mother every thirty seconds or so. Oh yeah... and I remember the tiered candles that sat in their little colored holders and the smell of burning incense, and who could ever forget all of that sitting and standing? I remember gazing up in awe at the large, wooden crucifix, situated high on the wall just beyond the altar. It always left me feeling a bit sad.

I vaguely remember going to Catechism and then to my "First Communion." The pictures in the family album tell the story best, especially the ones from my First Communion... There I am, with knobby knees and long, skinny legs at the bottom of my dove-white dress, my feet adorned in shiny, white patent leather shoes, a small, white lacy veil at my strawberry-blonde hair, and a freckled nose suspended just above my unsmiling lips. I'm sure that somewhere deep down I was grinning from ear to ear, anxious to dance up a storm with my Jesus in them there fancy white shoes... Regardless of how I might have felt about all the rigmarole, I'm sure I appreciated Jesus; anyone who took such good care of lambs must have been okay in my book.

There was Grace said before every meal, and I remember

Dad reading scripture to me. He would explain everything as he went along, as it was all rather confusing to me, and although I often remained none the wiser about God and his mysterious ways, I enjoyed every second of every minute spent with my father.

A Daredevil in the Making?

As far back as I can remember I have been competitive by nature. Thriving on being lavished with an abundance of love and affection, I often vied for my father's attention with my younger sister and older brother. Seemingly content on being mom's favorite daughter, my sister placed little emphasis on the competition; my poor brother on the other hand grew only more and more desperate, often acting up as a last-ditch effort to win some attention. More often than not he wound up with his nose out of joint. I must admit—I cared not one iota. My insatiable need for attention far outweighed any feelings of compassion I may otherwise have had for my dear brother!

I thoroughly enjoyed beating my brother, Jamie, and his friends at penny poker. Grinning from ear to ear, I'd scoop up my prized pile of shiny, copper coins to disappear before any of them had a chance to react. Whenever I would hear a game unfolding in our basement, I'd race down the steps as fast as my little feet would carry me, dash into the den, and adamantly refuse to leave until I'd won every penny. Tempers often flared, and my removal seemed at hand, but the fires of discontent were easily extinguished with threats of tattling on my brother's past misdeeds.

I loved playing games of chance, especially card games,

and became a fierce competitor. Relentlessly, I would torment my partner, insisting that we play again and again until I'd won the majority of games. It gave me a great sense of accomplishment to whip my Dad at Scrabble, as his vast vocabulary gave him such an advantage (who knew a zebu was a domesticated Asian or African bovine mammal with a prominent hump and a large dewlap??? And while we're at it... what the heck is a dewlap!? An ant's early morning jog around a blade of grass? Good golly...).

I had to be the first to have the training wheels removed from my bicycle, and suffered several mishaps as a result. The first occurred as I rode my "new and improved" bike down Overwaitea Hill. My dad traveled alongside me, coaching me as I went along. Soon, I began picking up speed, and before I knew it, I was racing full tilt down the town's longest hill. My father watched in horror as I lost control of the little, blue bike and went headfirst into the pavement.

I was quite proud of my wound, a mild concussion, and thoroughly enjoyed the extra attention I received from my parents during my recovery.

As a child, my greatest quest was to impress my father. I remember his face beaming with pride as I fearlessly jumped from the highest diving board at Radium Hot Springs' swimming pool when I was less than four feet tall. Dad rewarded my brave feat with a quarter, or "two bits" as he called it, just before he'd receive the inevitable tongue-lashing from the lifeguard. We usually got in two or three good dives before being kicked out altogether.

From the age of four to the age of ten, my closest companion, on the second rung of the ladder below my father of course, was a boy who shared my passion for performing daredevil feats. Conrad performed best when he took on the persona of his favorite super hero. Every fiber of his small, wiry frame became charged with superpower the moment he slipped into that electric blue cape. And it was Superman we blamed (or at least his defective cape) the day Conrad nearly killed himself attempting to fly off the garage roof. Still, we were a force to be reckoned with. Together Conrad and I rescued people in peril, you know, from car wrecks and burning buildings and such. Before long, my Dad had dubbed my fearless friend, "Hector the Protector." Although I too possessed superhero powers, my father still affectionately referred to me only as "Chick" (or Chick-chack, Chicory-chack, Triple Chick ...).

My friendship with Conrad was shed like a snake's skin when I entered grade six. So, too, it seems, were my superhero powers...

My very first sixth grade lesson was a painful one, taught not by the teacher, but by my fellow classmates. The subject: Peer Pressure.

Clad in a cute denim dress and with frilly, lace socks, I strolled into class that fateful first day. Being the daughter of the school principal had already labeled me a "goody-goody" and my prissy attire only confirmed it. Instantly, I became the laughingstock of my fellow sixth-graders who, if you'd asked me, appeared little more than a bunch of clones in their identical attire of denim jeans and tees.

I did not smoke cigarettes or marijuana. Strike two. And failing their sex quiz, well, that earned me strike three in a hurry. I was out. Nothing short of a personality transplant would be required for me to fit in now.

The following day, another new girl arrived to class. She wore faded jeans and a navy blue t-shirt, and although it took her some time to get over the nausea and fits of coughing, eventually she mastered the art of marijuana and cigarette smoking. Many years would pass before she was able to kick that dang tobacco habit...

Soon, I was also to discover the forbidden pleasures of kissing with my very first boyfriend. The great event took place shortly after I'd favorably answered his note, 'Will you go out with me? Check yes or no.' Even though going "all the way" was considered entirely cool at the ripe age of eleven, I managed to preserve my virginity until I was practically an old maid of fifteen.

During my teen years I pulled away from my father. Being doted on by a steady boyfriend and getting carried away with drugs and alcohol had become my priority. It was no small miracle that I survived skiing Black Diamond runs under the influence of LSD, and snorting cocaine until my nose bled.

My parents tried everything. At first, they approached me all calm, cool and collected, armed with a well-rehearsed lecture; this eventually turned into a whole lot of ranting and raving, which, in my opinion, made them appear as though they'd more than "located" my stash... And then came the silent treatment. This was, by far, the absolute worst. But I managed to persevere, defiant until the bitter end. I'm sure they prayed a thousand prayers during that time. I, on the other hand, was a tad too busy with a drink in the left and a joint in the right...

In Junior High my behaviors became even less godly. I became a bully. I'm not sure what possessed me to torment the less popular kids so mercilessly; it haunts me to this day. I shamefully recall one hapless victim in particular...

Poor Rebecca had flaming red hair, unruly and frightfully frizzy, making her an instant target for ridicule. She also had a "wandering eye," an unsightly birth defect that made it difficult for both of her eyes to focus simultaneously on any given object. Further "flattering" the girl's appearance was an unusually thick pair of corrective lenses. They quite literally appeared to have been fashioned from the bottoms of two soda-pop bottles. And it didn't end there; long, gangly limbs dangled from a disproportionately small torso, only to be topped off with a severely freckled face.

Not one student in the entire school bothered to find out who might be trapped beneath Rebecca's outer shell. Least of all, me...

As the timid girl made her way down the hall, she accidentally bumped into me. Being on one of my happy marijuana highs, it really didn't faze me... until I caught a glimpse of the hair, that is. I became infuriated, chasing after her to punch her squarely in the face. Rebecca's eyeglasses flew off her nose to land at her feet. I stood there, gazing down at the misshapen object as though entirely perplexed at how it might have gotten there. And then my buzz was gone and I was taken aback by my own behavior. This sudden attack of conscience was short lived, however, all but extinguished by the flood of approval washing over me. Delighted spectators laughed and cheered as redheaded Rebecca groped the floor in search of her glasses. Her sobbing only fueled the frenzy, initiating a game of soccer.

The school principal was not only outraged by the incident, but horribly humiliated as well. Likely because he was my father ...

When I hit Senior High, some of my personality traits underwent an about-face. I'm not sure what exactly inspired the transformation, but I am certain of one boy's appreciation of it.

Leon Leekmaster had to be the most unpopular boy in the entire school. 'He lives a few hours behind his mind,' the teachers explained to the student body, 'and he tries earnestly to catch up.' The kid might have stood a chance had they left it at that. But life can be cruel, so they quickly added 'Leon is a very nice boy who just needs special attention.' Well, special attention he got! At every opportunity, he was bombarded with spitballs and tripped in the hallway. To the already extraordinarily vast vocabulary of most students, the name Leon was added as a synonym for loser. Being labeled a "Leon" led to unbearable loneliness.

The hallway was littered with students, some with faces buried in textbooks, others offsetting the grueling task with some naughty necking. Hearing a commotion at the end of the hall, I hastened my pace to find out what the fuss was about.

There, sprawled out over the floor, was Leon, textbooks strewn from one side of the hallway to the other. Surrounding him was a mob of students grinning from ear to ear, as though they'd just accomplished some great feat. As I peered down at the fallen student, he looked up at me. Never before had I seen such a sad pair of eyes.

Something stirred within me, and before I knew it, I was freaking out—yelling at everyone to leave him the hell alone. Being a fairly popular student, my stance carried some weight. And from that day forward, Leon Leekmaster suffered very little, if any, bullying; in fact, he pretty much thrived over the next few years, lavished with that "special attention" he'd so desperately needed all along: Kindness.

I managed to maintain reasonable grades throughout High School, although they did not reflect my true potential, and followed my boyfriend to Calgary immediately after graduating in 1984. I just knew that somewhere there, amid the exciting hustle and bustle of big city life, my fame and fortune awaited me...

An Oversized Omen

Fortune found me not in Calgary but in Las Vegas. The year was 1989 when my boyfriend, Chase, and I accompanied his sister, Amanda, for a fun-filled excursion to the desert paradise. I was instantly captivated by the colorful city of lights, elated by the constant buzz of excitement seeping out from the casinos.

After a quick lesson on how to deposit coins and pull the lever of a "One-armed Bandit," I became all but oblivious to life around me. It was as though I'd entered a new dimension of reality, wandered across some invisible threshold to a magical realm where only my new friends and I existed. I thought of the slot machines not as mere inanimate objects, but rather like living "things" capable of stimulating interaction.

Drawn into the perpetual flow of colorful motion I soon found myself *inside* the machine. And it would be there, on a miniature stage, within the colorful screen of a Las Vegas slot machine, unbeknownst to me, that I would make my debut as a compulsive gambler.

It was entirely engrossing; the anticipation of a win was constant, gripping my senses with such intensity that I would nearly drown in adrenaline. A mere drop of a coin followed by a quick pull on a lever produced an instantaneous high.

Watching... waiting... pretty colors and shapes spinning, spinning... Oh, *please, please, please*...! It was like nothing I'd ever experienced before. It was as though I'd discovered a wonderful, new drug and could not get it into my veins fast enough.

My new friends and I were in the midst of getting acquainted when Chase and Amanda rudely intruded. They'd gotten into their heads some silly notion that I might want to join them for dinner. I found it extremely annoying to be torn away from the magical realm of slot machines to endure such mundane activity.

Evening found me in an utter state of euphoria, thoroughly enjoying my beginner's luck. I quickly graduated from little league (nickel slots) with a prosperous performance, earning the right to play in the big league (quarter slots). I traveled the entire circuit of gambling machines, carefully collecting each small fortune before moving on to my next conquest. I loved the sound of clanking coins as they came shooting out into the metal tray, enjoyed the envious looks from fellow players as the attention-grabbing noise hollered *Check it out, folks! Luck be the lady with the loudest machine!* I thrived on the exhilarating ambience of the casino, its ringing bells and flashing lights. Even the blue-gray haze of cigarette smoke appeared mystical.

Suddenly a great commotion began to unfold. I saw several people rushing towards one of the high-stakes blackjack tables, including four men in paramedic uniforms. The first two were yelling, "Clear the way, please! Clear the way!" while the pair on their heels carried a stretcher.

I joined several other patrons standing on tiptoe to catch sight of the unfortunate soul lying beside the blackjack table. It was strange, really—I didn't want to look... yet I just couldn't help myself.

The paramedics quickly surrounded the man and began to administer CPR. After some time, they stopped. An oxygen mask was placed over his ashen face, his overweight body lifted onto the stretcher, and moments later, the man was loaded into the waiting ambulance.

"Dear God, I hope he pulls through," I heard a woman say.

"I wonder what happened to him," I heard myself utter.

"Well, it had to be one of two things, I'd imagine," the woman replied. "Either he was overly excited by a big win, or devastated by a big loss."

I was left feeling a bit queasy by the whole incident, but managed to resume playing my slot machine.

(In retrospect, I can't help but wonder if the ordeal had been an omen, the warning sign I'd disregarded until it was much too late.)

I was delighted to discover that the casinos of Las Vegas never sleep, as sleep was the furthest thing from my mind. (Years later, I was told that extra oxygen is pumped into the casinos' ventilation systems to keep visitors energized and ready to gamble at all hours of the day and night. I do not know for certain whether or not this is true, but I must say, I find it awfully easy to believe...)

I did not retire until late morning the following day, and still only managed a couple hours' sleep. I'm almost certain it was a one-armed bandit who tapped me on the shoulder to rouse me back to consciousness... And I could hardly wait to find him, grab hold of that arm of his, and yank on it a good dozen or so times—at least until it yielded me a fortune. But hunger somehow prevailed, and before I knew it, I had joined Chase and Amanda for lunch.

Short of visiting a washroom or retreating to one's hotel room, there was simply no escaping the gambling frenzy. The same exhilarating atmosphere flowed through the open restaurant, tempting diners to place a bet even while breaking for a bite to eat. Keno cards sat on every table, making it ever so convenient. Relief for indigestion should also have been provided with meals being so hastily ingested by gamblers anxious to return to the main battlefield.

My winning streak continued for the duration of our stay, interrupted only by the occasional meal and siesta.

The flight home was extremely turbulent. A young girl stirred panic among the passengers, wailing relentlessly until the bouncing plane found its way to smoother skies. Pale green faces of hung-over casino dwellers expressed regret for taking advantage of the constant flow of complimentary alcohol the night before. In all fairness, the scantily clad barmaids likely deserved a share of the blame.

As the plane touched down in Calgary, immediately, I began to feel glum. I missed the adrenaline pumping through my veins, the anticipation of the big win, the sound of clanking coins. But most of all, I missed my temporary retreat from reality. I was not looking forward to returning to work, or much else in my boring, old life for that matter. Before I had my seatbelt unfastened, I'd already planned my next trip to Vegas. (As it would turn out, however, I'd be forced to make do with the remote chance of selecting a winning set of numbers on Lotto 6-49, or striking it rich yelling, "Bingo!")

My next travel adventure with Amanda took us sightseeing in Budapest and wandering through the eerie maze of catacombs embedded beneath Rome. We gazed in awe at Michelangelo's masterpiece mural adorning the domed ceiling of Rome's most famous Cathedral, and stood on the stone balcony of Romeo's beloved Juliet, in Verona. Our gondola guide pointed out the former home of the infamous Casanova as we glided through the canals of Venice, and we became smitten under the romantic spell of Italy. We gazed nostalgically at the ruins of ancient Pompeii, and were especially touched by the petrified remains of a most unfortunate dog, chained to a post and apparently writhing in agony as it met its fate in the oozing lava having erupted from Mount Vesuvius almost 2000 years ago. A young boy sat nearby, face buried in his hands, perhaps turned to stone with his unbearable grief just moments after an unsuccessful attempt to save his beloved dog.

Although I thoroughly enjoyed my European vacation —filled with unforgettable, once-in-a-lifetime experiences— fonder memories remained for me in Las Vegas.

A PLACE WHERE WEEDS & ROSES GROW

Sleepless in Mexico

Blessed with a friend employed by a large airline, Amanda soon received three more airline tickets, this time to the tropical paradise of Cancun, Mexico. The only hitch was that the plane made its departure out of Vancouver, with a one-night stopover in Colorado. (Never mind the little detour; had I any inkling of how "crazy" the trip would ultimately become, likely I would have thought twice about going at all.)

Amanda, her cousin, Charlotte, and I set out for Vancouver in the dead of winter. We managed to keep warm with thoughts of escaping the snow and freezing temperatures.

I remember wishing that the pilot would make a drastic error and land in Vegas, but no such luck. As the aircraft made its descent into Cancun, however, I was immediately drawn to the splendor awaiting us. My heart fluttered as I peered down at the endless sea of blue glittering in the sunlight, as though home to the world's finest diamonds. As the shoreline crept into view, I could almost feel the cool, sandy beach at my feet. A shiver of excitement found me, cloaking my body in gooseflesh and turning my lips into the silliest of grins.

We checked into an exquisite beachfront hotel and got changed into our swimsuits. After slathering suntan lotion onto our pasty white bodies, we headed out into the scorching sun.

We lazed around, baking in the heat, sipping exotic drinks adorned with miniature umbrellas. Later, we joined in a game of beach volleyball and took a dip in the ocean.

Early evening found us wandering from kiosk to kiosk, admiring the endless array of wares. Radiant smiles beamed at us from friendly brown faces as voices bellowed, "Hey Senoritas! Have I got a deal for you! Come see my beautiful jewelry! Come see my beautiful dresses! Look! This one was made for you!"

The mouth-watering aroma of fresh lobster and crab was more than we could bear after working up ravenous appetites bartering with the Mexicans. After gorging ourselves on the succulent seafood, we headed back to the hotel to try on our new dresses. For our evening out I selected the white cotton, off-the-shoulder dress that so nicely complimented my newly tanned skin.

We wandered along the main strip of Cancun without a care in the world, the warm island breeze playfully tousling our hair. Gazing skyward, we strolled along, each of us lost in our own thoughts as the sun surrendered its pastel pinks to the moon's enchanting glow.

Near-darkness fell, and before long, we found ourselves drawn to the magical beginnings of the island's nightlife. We followed the sound of music to a club on the beach and ventured inside. It was jam-packed with tourists eager to party and hospitable locals eager to accommodate. There was music and dancing, and Tequila at every turn.

A good-looking guy of Spanish descent approached and invited me to join him on the dance floor. Immediately, our bodies found the rhythm and song after song we danced. We talked and laughed and enjoyed each other immensely.

Suddenly I was surrounded by a group of people, a long silver spout in my face. They began to stamp their feet and clap their hands, chanting in unison, "Drink! Drink! Drink! Drink!" So I did. The bearer of the giant keg positioned the spout an inch or so above my mouth and, pressing a button, yelled, "Go!" I gulped down as much of the tangy concoction as I could before the coughing and sputtering took over. My eyes watered as the strong liquid coated my throat, the pit of my stomach warming as the Tequila settled there.

My new friend and I danced until our legs would work no more, and then slowly made our way back to the table. I introduced to Amanda and Charlotte my handsome dance partner, butchering the poor guy's name all to pieces with my ridiculous attempt at a Spanish accent. It came out as "Lewy," as in Donald Duck's third nephew, only with a stronger emphasis on the "y" part.

I nearly drowned in Tequila that night. Not only did the keg find me every time I ventured out onto the dance floor, but a steady supply of "Tequila Whammies" made their way to our table as well. The drink server would "wham" the shooter onto the table, causing the lemony potion to start fizzing; thereby challenging the drinker to gulp it down before it overflowed. Another popular shooter was the "Slammer." Although the wee glass of clear liquid appeared harmless it was actually a well-disguised potent potable guaranteed to send you soaring. Now, the customary way to consume a Slammer was to lick the sprinkle of salt from the little flap of skin between forefinger and thumb, "slam" the liquid into the mouth, swallowing it in one brave gulp, and then suck on a slice of lemon. I practiced this feat until I had it down to an art form.

Sometime in the wee hours of morning Amanda and Charlotte announced through thick tongues that they were heading back to the hotel. I felt surprisingly sober for someone who had consumed enough Tequila to suffer alcohol poisoning.

I begged Amanda and Charlotte to stay, suggesting that they step outside for a breath of fresh air to revive themselves, but they insisted they were done. Before they walked away, they reminded me of the eventful itinerary planned for the following day. We intended to rise early and take in the sights, climb the pyramids of the Mayan Ruins and check out the sea life in our attractive ensemble of flippers and snorkels, all the while capturing each moment on film.

Though somewhat wary, Amanda and Charlotte had agreed that I could stay a while longer with the condition that Lewy escort me to the hotel afterwards. Amanda in particular had her reservations... Might have had something to do with the fact that I was still dating her brother.

We danced and drank for a time and then, although not the least bit fatigued, I insisted I retire to the hotel for a few hours rest before tackling the day's itinerary. Reluctantly, my friend agreed.

The hotel was located just off the main strip a short distance from the nightclub. As we began the short trek, Lewy decided to make one last-ditch effort to convince me to stay longer. Reaching out, he grabbed hold of my arm, turning me towards him in an attempt to sway me with his pleading eyes. I shook my head "no." And then the car was upon us, the sound of screeching tires freezing us in our tracks. Two police officers jumped out and with no warning whatsoever began an onslaught of punching and kicking with Lewy on the receiving end. He fell to the ground facedown, wrapping his arms about his head as the officers carried out their vicious assault. I stood there dumbfounded for several seconds before throwing myself overtop of Lewy. An inadvertent blow struck my lower back and for a horrifying moment I thought I, too, would be beaten to a pulp. Sobbing and near breathless, I somehow managed to holler, "Please stop! Please stop!"

As abruptly as the attack began, it stopped. One of the police officers asked me why I was protecting my "attacker." I just stared at him, unable to comprehend his question. He pointed a finger at Lewy, who remained on the ground, but now peered cautiously at us from the underside of an arm still stretched protectively over his head. "Was this guy not bothering you just moments ago?" he said, more as a statement than a question. I realized then that, from their perspective, the moment in which Lewy had grabbed my arm to turn me towards him, it must have appeared an assault on a treasured tourist was in the making. I let out a sigh of relief, even managed a small smile as I explained to the officers that that was not at all the case, that Lewy and I were in fact friends and he'd intended me no harm whatsoever.

After a brief huddle the police apologized for the misunderstanding and helped my friend to his feet. I was surprised he could stand at all. Then, as quickly as they'd come, they were gone, speeding off into the night as though making haste might erase the unfortunate event.

I slept not a wink—not an overly large surprise, really, considering the incident I'd just witnessed... But then, as I showered and dressed and readied myself for the day's endeavors, I felt an incredible surge of energy flow through my body. Logic told me I should be exhausted not to mention suffering a severe hangover, but I felt nothing of the sort. In fact, I felt the complete opposite...

I clambered up the pyramids as though they were oversized anthills, including the steepest, which bore a sixty-degree incline. The towering structure was equipped with a thick chain that ran up the center of its stone staircase, a helping hand for those perhaps a tad less invincible.

Peering down at the ground from atop the pyramid produced a dizzying effect. I couldn't help but wonder how many had fallen to their death, accidentally or otherwise. I backed away from the edge. For me, the descent proved more difficult than the climb, and by the time my foot found the ground, I was glad it was over.

We snorkeled through the warm waters, gazing in wonder at the exotic sea life. Hidden just beneath the water's surface was a most spectacular scene, made up of vibrantly colored fish, slow-ambling starfish and spiny creatures with protruding eyeballs. Causing the sandy floor to appear "alive" were crustaceans of every shape and size, each with a shack on its back, some speckled, some freckled, some bedazzled in jewels... or were those fancy barnacles? In any case, each and every one possessed a very busy set of legs scampering this way and that way, all in a seemingly endless search for just the right spot to call home.

Poor Amanda experienced great difficulty in using her breathing apparatus. I'm not sure what the problem was, but every thirty seconds or so she'd begin gagging and choking to the point of almost vomiting. The large, rubber flippers attached to her feet only enhanced Amanda's less than graceful performance, and with each mouthful of water, her oversized feet would begin to flounder. Seconds later, she'd be thrashing all about, arms flailing, and water splashing in every direction. It appeared as though she was making her debut (and quite an impressive one at that!) as the "main course" in the next "Jaws" sequel. I laughed so hard that I, too, began to take in water. She did eventually get the hang of it, but by then, the frightened sea creatures had all gone into hiding.

As we entered the hotel lobby, I spotted Lewy lounging in an overstuffed chair. He wore shorts and a muscle shirt, and a smile that made me smile right back. As I walked towards him, immediately I noticed the bruising. It was pretty hard to miss, really. Virtually every inch of his exposed skin told the tale.

As Lewy attempted to stand, he winced in pain. The culprit: two broken ribs. I was amazed at the amount of damage the officers were able to inflict in such a short period of time. But Lewy was a trooper, refusing to complain one iota about the ordeal.

That evening he joined us for a pirate ship excursion to a smaller island located just off the coast of Cancun. It was great fun. Our hosts went all out, making the experience as convincing as possible. They appeared the real deal, complete with scruffy beards and eye patches, each brandishing a silver-bladed sword, glinting with such sinister intentions that nervous giggles could be heard rippling out over the water. We purchased souvenir photos of the menacing pirates with their swords at our throats... *my* Jack Sparrow having gone so far as to grab a handful of hair, pulling my head back to ready my juglar for that one quick pull of the blade...

Soon, we, too, had rum on our breath (and tequila... always lots of tequila!). We could not have been in greater spirits as we took in the island's festivities. First there came the bronze-skinned dancers, each painted in ancient tribal markings and topped off with elaborate headwear. Hot on their trail were the fire-dancers, and then a little more rum (and tequila!) and it was time for some limbo. Thank goodness for soft, merciful sand...

Before their heads hit the pillows, my girlfriends were fast asleep, while I remained wide-eyed and ready for more. I stared up at the familiar ceiling, overflowing with energy, wound up with a restlessness that seemed a permanent part of me now. I tossed and turned... and then tossed and turned. Finally, I jumped up, threw on some shorts and a tank top, and headed for the door.

The moon was aglow, surrounded in silver specks blinking and winking a secret language entirely their own. There's nothing like a moonlit walk on the soft-sand beaches of far away, waves lapping at your toes, a warm, salty breeze at your face. Without a care in the world I sauntered along, kicking playfully at the water's edge.

I traveled a fair distance before turning around. Immediately, a wave of panic found me, as I gazed at the vast array of hotels dotting the beach. Each appeared identical to the next... just another, and another, and another in an endless string of fallen stars twinkling mischievously in the far-off darkness.

And then from somewhere under the night sky, there came a faint voice. As it grew louder, I recognized it to be Amanda's. For once I welcomed the familiar sound of motherly concern, my fears subsiding altogether as her silhouette materialized in the near distance. I ran over to greet her, only to be scolded for wandering off alone in the dead of night. But I didn't mind.

After another failed attempt to find sleep I sneaked out of the room a second time, this time clad in bikini. I dived into the hotel's swimming pool with the intention of tiring myself out with a few laps, but before I got halfway through the first one, I was being fished out by hotel security. Apparently the pool hours were not designed with insomniac guests in mind.

The eve of our departure from Vancouver to Cancun had been a restless one for me; I'd lain awake half the night before in eager anticipation of our fun-in-the-sun getaway. The following night in Cancun was entirely without sleep (not at all surprising after the horror show I'd witnessed), and then the third night was spent frolicking about the beaches and attempting to swim a marathon. So in a span of approximately sixty hours, I'd slept maybe six, and yet felt inexplicably energized. *Must be the humidity reacting with the alcohol,* I mused to myself.

I finally caught a couple hours' sleep before joining Amanda and Charlotte for breakfast. The main topic of conversation over the morning meal: my sudden inability to sleep like a normal human being. I also received two motherly lectures on the dangers of a young woman wandering alone at night in a foreign country.

The remainder of our stay was filled with exciting activities such as drinking Tequila, sightseeing, drinking Tequila, swimming, dancing, eating seafood, and... drinking Tequila. I averaged a mere two to three hours' sleep per night, yet felt invigorated beyond belief. It was like being on a super duper cocaine high, only... without the cocaine!

I knew it was odd for me not to be succumbing to the lack of sleep, as I'd always required seven or eight hours to function optimally; but somehow I dismissed my concerns with a logical explanation that the thrills of the adventure were simply overriding any need for sleep. Besides, had I not encountered a similar experience in Las Vegas?

As we boarded the plane bound for our former lives, I desperately wished we could stay another week. It was difficult to tell Lewy goodbye, as I'd fallen head over heels in love with him. But, after a lengthy embrace, I managed to pull away.

I gazed out the window at the happy island below and as it grew smaller and smaller, wondered if Lewy felt as heartbroken as I did.

5

Cocktails & Catamarans

Our overnight stay in Houston, Texas en route to Vancouver was entirely uneventful. Except, of course, for all the weird and wonderful things that took place...

Late evening found me pacing the floor of our hotel room while Amanda and Charlotte slumbered peacefully. I'd made an honest attempt to join them in Dreamland but apparently it wasn't meant to be. So I made my way to the terrace, gazing up to once again find the heavens filled with silver specks busily conversing about God only knows what.

I giggled aloud as I said, "Are you there, God? It's me, Joan." And with that, a group of stars began moving about in the sky, and within seconds, had formed a brilliant constellation of letters. I could not believe my eyes as I read the words: Well, hello there, Joan. It's me, God.

Okay, okay... Nothing quite so profound happened. But I did feel the presence of something unusual. Hard to describe, really, but one thing is for certain, it was unlike anything I'd encountered before. It was sort of like how I might imagine an electric surge to be if it were buzzing about beneath my skin. I felt tingly all over. It was a lot like being cloaked in extra large gooseflesh, only... entirely different. It felt as though I were being touched, soft as a whisper, caressed by the aura of someone or something I could sense but not quite see. It was very strange, not in an unpleasant way, and I missed it immediately when it ended.

I conversed with God a bit longer, puffing away on a cigarette while sharing with him my desire to quit smoking. I concluded my chat with the Almighty by confessing that I really didn't know whether or not I still believed in his existence, 'no offence or anything'... And then, as I turned to walk away, I decided spur of the moment to toss up the idea that he might want to show me "some kind of sign"...

I half-expected a shooting star to slice through the night sky, or an earth-shattering clap of thunder to stir my unconscious friends... But again, nothing quite so profound...

I managed a brief nap before it was time to rise and shine. After showering and dressing, I began a great search for my lighter. I was looking so forward to that first cigarette of the day. Amanda had misplaced her lighter as well, and Charlotte merely bummed a smoke now and then, so neither carried a book of matches. And the lack of the customary packet served up in the hotel's imitation crystal ashtray must have been an oversight on the chambermaid's part.

After searching high and low and to and fro without success, I concluded God was the culprit. Obviously he'd taken to heart my little comment about quitting and had hid my lighter. I chuckled at the notion.

Immediately after breakfast I proceeded to chain-smoke, lighting the first with a match from a packet inscribed with *Smitty's Pancake House*. Although my headache worsened with each additional cigarette, I smiled at each and every smoke ring as it floated on up to Heaven.

A large family sat at a table next to us. Mealtime appeared quite the ordeal with each of three young children needing help to dress their pancakes while an even younger sibling launched missiles of unwanted food from atop his high chair. "Bombs away!" his giggles seemed to say.

As we passed by the busy family on our way out, I impulsively stopped at their table, smiled at the parents and said, "God bless you and your children!" They smiled nervously, perhaps expecting me to carry on with a sermon of some sort. Amanda and Charlotte looked mortified.

We were last to board the plane to Vancouver. Only single seating remained, so I found myself seated amid two strangers. After a quick introduction I came to learn that although the two women were travel companions, they'd decided to leave the seat between them vacant. Caroline, to my left, preferred the aisle seat while Nancy, to my right, preferred the window seat. I was certain I liked the middle seat least of all, but apparently that was beside the point.

The tanned pair had just enjoyed a two-week stay in Cancun also, and was now headed back to their home in Vancouver.

As discretely as possible, I set out to study my new acquaintances, first one, and then the other. (I smiled sweetly on the two occasions where I was caught... first by one, and then the other.) Nancy appeared quiet and thoughtful; her eyes a gentle fawn color, with long, sweeping lashes that seemed to go on forever. She was a natural beauty; I could detect only a hint of mascara with a smidgen of pale pink rouge, and just enough flesh-tone lip-gloss to enhance a pair of already sensuous lips. Her hair looked so soft I was tempted to reach out and touch it. Her voice was equally soft, so hushed in fact, that I had to strain my ear to catch her every word.

Caroline could not have been more different with her short, dark hair, spiked on top and appearing almost lacquered in spots; perhaps an extra gob of gel had been required to do battle with the island's early-morning humidity. Her voice was deep and raspy, manly almost, but as she fidgeted with the pamphlets peeking out from the pocket at the back of the seat before her, complaining all the while of a "nicotine fit," I decided her vocal cords were just swimming in tar. Momentarily, I was reminded of how much I'd come to want to quit the habit.

Although the two were near polar opposites, unlikely friends at best, I liked them both immediately; and as they began sharing with me stories of their adventure, I became captivated by one of Caroline's tales in particular...

"Side by side we were sailing, catamarans gliding over the gentle waves, when out from nowhere appeared a speedboat. It was looming directly towards us, and moving at a pretty good clip. As it grew dangerously close, Nancy began to scream, and seconds later, she was forced to abandon her catamaran. I was left sailing solo, struggling to steer my little vessel out of harm's way. I have to admit I was pretty scared. I tried desperately to force enough wind into the sail to alter my course, probably even tried blowing on the stupid thing myself, but to no avail. The wind had died down to a faint breeze.

"As the boat grew larger I thought I'd have a heart attack, the roar of its engine so deafeningly loud that I barely heard Nancy's frantic pleas for me to jump. Not that it mattered anyway, as I was pretty much paralyzed with fear by now. And then her voice stopped... Nancy had folded her hands in prayer to earnestly beg the Lord to spare us.

"At the last second, I closed my eyes and held my breath, bracing myself for death. And then there was silence. Slowly, I raised my eyelids, and as I began to breathe again, was shocked to discover myself alive... and with all body parts intact! My eyes found Nancy in the near distance, bobbing in the water, safe and sound.

"We both scanned the water's surface, but all we found were several boats in the far off distance, crawling leisurely across the horizon."

Tears welled in both women's eyes as the one recounted their tale. Of course, Caroline immediately did away with hers, while her more sensitive counterpart allowed each and every tear to tumble freely down a soft, pink cheek. And the moment the story was finished, in perfect unison, the pair shrugged their shoulders and shook their heads.

I couldn't help but wonder—for just a moment or two —what Caroline might have looked like in a bikini...

Truly I'd been spellbound, but nevertheless, I concluded the twosome were either the world's greatest storytellers or a pair of party girls having consumed an unusually potent batch of cocktails just prior to setting sail.

A PLACE WHERE WEEDS & ROSES GROW

6

An Ancient Belle in Black

Upon arrival in Vancouver, Amanda, Charlotte and I decided to grab some breakfast before starting the long drive home to Calgary. We wound up in a quaint little café seated at a small wooden table. We pretty much had our pick of the bunch, as there were no other patrons in sight. There were two chairs at the one side of the table we'd chosen, and a long, continuous bench at the opposite side, which ran the length of the wall, cleverly accommodating a string of closely-knit tables. Charlotte sat solo, while Amanda joined me on the bench.

As we ate breakfast we reminisced about our excursion, and although the conversation was engaging, it was impossible not to be distracted by the coffee. It was so bad the three of us had to wonder if it was leftover from the day before. Reminded me of the stuff commonly put on rooftops —"Tar," I believe the popular term to be. Oh, well. The extra jolt of caffeine would do us good. We had quite the long journey ahead of us, after all.

We'd just finished our meals and were in the process of accepting refills of the tar, when I noticed a woman entering the restaurant. Our eyes met as she ambled in our direction, and did not part ways until she'd passed by a number of vacant tables. Even then, my eyes were to drift only slightly upward.

I was astounded by the woman's height; she appeared well over six feet tall. Sure I'd seen women of considerable height before—models, basketball players—I'd just never seen one quite so *unbelievable*. Wrinkle upon wrinkle upon wrinkle, yet she displayed not the slightest trace of the hunched back typically associated with a person having survived an entire century. No eyeglasses, no cane, no nothing. I couldn't help but think to myself, *this woman's mismatched body parts appear to have been put together by some sort of prankster! Yikes!* And then my thoughts turned to regret, as she seemed to peer more deeply into my eyes; I felt certain that she was viewing my thoughts, taking in the newly fashioned (perhaps less than flattering) portrait of herself. I'm sure I looked away for a moment. And then a sigh of relief, as I recognized only pure kindness coming from her steady gaze.

With only kind judgement in my heart now, I continued to examine the fascinating woman headed my way. It was so strange; the place was not particularly spacious, and my new friend was traveling at a fairly regular pace (if not faster, with those incredibly long legs), and yet it seemed I had all the time in the world to take an inventory before she'd ever complete her journey.

Dressed entirely in black, she appeared as though she might be in mourning. An outdated pillbox sat atop her carefully coifed silver hair, complementing a full-length, charcoal-colored coat from which a pair of black boots emerged. The coat was made of some sort of material that reminded me of a black wooly lamb.

After sweeping the aged woman from head to toe, my eyes came to rest on her well-worn boots. I pondered the scuffmarks, my imagination kicking into gear, spinning a tale of a lonely old soul with nothing better to do than wander aimlessly about town marking up her once shiny boots. Her apparent age lent credence to the notion, making it entirely feasible for her to have outlived a husband and any other loved ones she may have had. Maybe she really was in mourning... A pang of sadness found my heart, and a moment later I felt a lump catch at my throat.

Completely engrossed in the tale, I continued to stare at the battered boots until they suddenly stopped before me. Slowly, I lifted my gaze to find the most riveting blue eyes I had ever seen. Actually they were more of a gray-blue, and even more probing now as they peered down at me from within that intricate web of wrinkles they called home. The strangeness continued to play over my senses; instantly, I became self-conscious, *painfully* self-conscious, while at the same time, overwhelmed with a longing to reveal my *entire being* to this stranger.

"May I sit there beside you?" I heard the woman ask. Although I could plainly see that she was aiming her question at me, it took me some time to respond.

"Uh, yes...yes of course," I said at last, letting out the very long breath I hadn't realized I'd been holding. And with that, the old woman slid onto the bench to settle in a mere foot or so from me. She removed her hat and placed it on the seat next to her, where I could no longer see it.

"Feels like more snow is coming," she said, as she removed her black gloves to place them neatly at the table's edge. I glanced down at her hands, expecting to find them gnarled and ridden with arthritis, but all I found was a pair of regular looking hands, unscathed and slightly wrinkled. Perhaps Palmolive, the dish detergent "for younger looking hands," was their saving grace. Not a single ring adorned the long, graceful fingers.

My gaze returned to the woman's face, and as I began to examine the countless creases and lines that went this way and that way, I felt as though I were reading a story. I saw times of loss and sorrow, a grief so unbearable it pained me just to witness it, and then a gathering of playful crinkles about her eyes, telling me of great joy. I could almost hear a child's giggles, and then a young woman's laughter, the sigh of true love and a wee babe's first cries. And then more sadness... I was certain her entire life was written there.

The waitress placed a cup and saucer with matching teapot before my well-preserved friend and moments later delivered a blueberry scone. The old woman poured a cup of the steaming hot tea and gingerly dipped her pastry. As she ate, I decided to study her facial profile. I couldn't help myself; the longing for more of that fascinating tale was more than I could bear. I just knew I was meant to learn as much as possible about this wonderfully strange woman. But for some reason, I found it near impossible to read her story from this new perspective. In an unvoiced whisper, I gently pleaded with her, asked her to turn her face back toward mine. I was hoping she would again read my thoughts; but she did not respond right away.

Was that a hint of a smile? A mischievous grin, almost? I couldn't be sure.

Amanda, being the appointed driver for our long trek home to Calgary, intended to drink an entire pot of coffee before heading out. She and Charlotte were deep in conversation over her fourth cup, and thus far, had barely acknowledged the woman next to me.

"You know what?" I heard the old woman say. "You should accept Jesus Christ into your heart." As I turned to gaze into her eyes, I was a little taken aback by what I found. There was a sophisticated wisdom intertwined with a child-like innocence, perhaps the gray blending with the blue, and the longer I looked, the more familiar it all became. *Do I know you?* I wanted to say. But the words wouldn't come.

A strange sensation came over me, not unpleasant, but definitely out of the ordinary. It's difficult to describe, really, but I suppose if I were to try I might liken it to a gentle current of electricity humming through my veins causing every hair on my body to stand on end. Like "the shivers," only not the cold, creepy kind. It was not unlike the sensation I'd experienced the night before on the hotel balcony.

"I've already accepted Jesus," I heard my voice say.

"Oh?" countered the old woman. "Have you really now?"

"Well... Yes," I said. "My parents go to church, and I used to go to church, and *sometimes I still pray.*"

"Praying is a good thing," she advised, in a tone rich with praise. Her words made me feel warm inside. I was, however, entirely unprepared for the woman's next remark, as she looked me in the eye and said:

"Jesus is black."

I tried to make sense of her words, wondered if she'd perhaps meant to say "back." After all, I could recall not one picture depicting Jesus as anything other than a bearded Caucasian. When I finally said, "What do you mean?" she merely repeated the words, saying:

"Jesus is black."

The woman then took a final sip of her tea and smiled,

slipped her hands into the leather gloves patiently waiting for her and stood up. "Well, I best be on my way now," she said. A blanket of sadness fell over me. It felt cold and lonely, but I did not protest. Secretly, I hoped she would forget her hat. But at the last...possible...moment... she reached down to retrieve it from the seat. Again... *was that a mischievous grin?*

As my tall friend walked away, I turned to Charlotte and Amanda. "Did you hear all that?!" I practically shouted.

Charlotte, a stern Atheist, replied, simply, "Yeah. Jesus is black. Maybe they tarred and feathered him and all the feathers fell off."

I didn't bother to reply.

Downing the last of my now lukewarm coffee, I headed for the Ladies' Room. Then, while Amanda took care of the bill, I wandered out into the freezing cold. I closed my eyes to receive winter's caress on my face, the wind so shockingly cold and abrasive I found it more like an abusive slap. I struggled to catch my breath. And then the wind died down and as the subtle scent of snow took over my senses, I was reminded of the old woman's forecast.

I glanced to the right of me, and then the left; and there she was... *the ancient belle in black.*

The distinct figure, about a block and a half or so up the sidewalk, turned to wave at me. But before I had a chance to return the gesture, she'd turned back around to continue into the distance. And then it dawned on me. *She must have left the restaurant a good fifteen minutes ago. How could she possibly have known the exact moment I would look at her? This simply cannot be...*

Slowly, I scanned my surroundings. Not another soul to be found. *Odd, for a city street*, I thought to myself. I returned my gaze to the old woman. Still unable to fathom the situation, I closed my eyes to erase the silly illusion. It worked! Sort of ... The image was merely diminished in size, shrinking one coat size at a time as it slowly sauntered into the distance.

Momentarily, I turned my head, as Charlotte and Amanda stepped out from the café. I returned my gaze to the old woman, forefinger poised. I was planning to point her out to Charlotte and Amanda, ask them what they thought of the whole thing. But my old woman was gone. I explained the event to my friends anyway, and then, with hands planted at my hips, said, in a most smart-ass tone, "Now what do you have to say for yourself, Char?"

"Well... I'm thinking maybe the old lady's a stalker!"

With that, I turned and headed for the car.

The snow fell hard and fast and made it difficult to see the road, but Amanda's T-Bird stayed the course, determined to wind its way, albeit ever so slowly, through the long and increasingly treacherous Roger's Pass. Amanda was at the wheel, I in the passenger seat, and Charlotte sprawled over the backseat.

"Better buckle up," Amanda told the rear-view mirror. Charlotte took her advice, but did not miss a beat in our conversation. We'd been debating the existence of God, playfully batting that ancient ball of opposition back and forth. I remember our voices sounding eerily muffled in the snow-covered mountains. Similar, I suppose, to what a call for help in an avalanche might be like.

Amanda had slowed the car to a mere crawl and was

straining against her seatbelt, jutting her neck toward the windshield in an attempt to gain a better view of the road. "You guys buckled up?" she asked. I could tell she was nervous. I, on the other hand, was finding it all quite exhilarating. It felt as though we were preparing to play some awesome new video game or something.

"Oh, not to worry, Amanda ... God will get us home safely!" I replied, looking to Charlotte for a reaction. She laughed as she checked her seatbelt, suggesting I might want to do the same "just in case God is busy." Amanda let out a sigh of annoyance.

The heavily treaded tires trudged along at a snail's pace. It was a near whiteout, and Amanda was beginning to show signs of exhaustion. I stared out past the waving windshield wipers to the falling flakes, watched in wonder as each found its place amid the infinite collage of white.

Suddenly Charlotte let out a great sneeze, startling Amanda and me out of our wits. It was so loud I thought she must have exaggerated the effect. *Hmmm... Two can play that game...* A mischievous smirk spread over my lips as I cranked my head around and said, "God bless you!" As the inevitable follow-up sneeze sounded, again I tossed Charlotte one of God's blessings.

"Would you guys cut it out?! I'm driving in a damn blizzard here in case you hadn't noticed!"

Amanda's outburst startled the both of us. I apologized while Charlotte tried unsuccessfully to stifle a third sneeze. I couldn't help myself. Slowly, I turned my face toward the backseat and, cupping my hand against my cheek to obscure Amanda's view, whispered softly, "God bless you." With that, a tiny giggle escaped Charlotte, re-igniting Amanda's anger.

"That's it!" she hollered, cranking the wheel towards the side of the road. Or at least what I'd *hoped* would be the side of the road. It was near impossible to tell with all the snow.

"We're going to sit here until you two children grow the hell up. In the meantime let's hope nobody happens by to knock us over the cliff." And with that said, Amanda closed her eyes and reclined her seat.

Humbled and a little bewildered, Charlotte and I exchanged a look of "oops-a-daisy" before slumping down in our seats. Neither of us knew quite what to do. So we did nothing. Just sat there, listening to the silence, Amanda with her eyes clamped shut, lips drawn into a tight, angry line, Charlotte and I gazing wide-eyed out the window like a couple of kids who'd never witnessed a snowfall. And as the seemingly endless assortment of flakes collected on the windshield, I wondered how long it would be before we were buried alive.

The faint red glow of a passerby's taillights came into view. I turned to Amanda, relieved to find that she, too, had taken notice. She turned the ignition switch to the on position and followed after the lights, grateful to have found a guide to get us through the snowstorm.

Charlotte and I resumed our friendly debate on the existence of God while Amanda concentrated on getting us home in one piece. Seconds later, Charlotte's sneezing resumed. She did her best to conceal each eruption, while I did my best to keep the giggles at bay.

She must be allergic to God, I decided.

We survived the long, trying trip to Calgary, arriving in the wee hours of morning.

A Story Without End

Chase was away on a fishing trip, expected to return home in a few days. I didn't mind so much that he wasn't there to greet me, as it would allow me some uninterrupted time to unwind and settle back into regular life. The two of us lived together in the basement of his sister's home, a spacious two-story tucked away snug in the cul-de-sac of a tranquil neighborhood in southeast Calgary.

I awoke with boundless energy after sleeping just a brief few hours. Leaping out of bed, I clambered up the stairs so fast that I nearly fell face-first onto the landing. I put a pot of coffee on to brew and began pacing the floor, anxious for Chase's call to arrive.

As expected, the telephone sounded at precisely nine o'clock. I rattled on and on, providing my boyfriend a play-by-play of my entire island adventure. Chase listened intently to my stories, especially the one about dancing the night away with Lewy, and then, the second I paused to catch my breath, he asked to speak with his sister. Amanda, likely awakened by the ringing of the telephone, had made her way down the stairs to join me for coffee. Yawning, she reached out and took the phone from me.

I immediately grew suspicious when I heard her say, "I think she's okay. Why? Oh. Well...yeah...maybe a little..." But what really got me going is the way she gawked at me the whole time.

The quaint little exchange was soon being wrapped up in a few "Uh-huh's," accompanied by the occasional side-glance in my direction. Being the topic of a conversation to which I was not entirely privy—especially one taking place directly before me—irked me to no end.

Amanda concluded her end of the conversation with a jovial, "Okey-dokey, then! See you soon!" and hung up the telephone.

Several silent moments passed.

"Oh...yeah..." she said, a little too absently. "He told me to tell you he's on his way home." She examined her fingernails as she spoke... first one and then another... and another... managing *oh-so-cleverly* to avoid eye contact with me.

"I thought he was staying a couple more days," I replied, whipping my hand up in an exaggerated fashion to start an intense examination of my own fingernails. "Your brother *loves* fishing... Do tell... What made him change his mind, Amanda?"

I knew something was up. That much was obvious. But what?

Silence.

I exhaled a long, slow breath of hot air to fog up my fingernails before polishing them to a shine on my shirt.

And then... time to cut to the chase.

"Amanda, what's going on?" I asked, my eyes narrowing into tiny slits of accusation.

As though having been nipped in the behind by some ravenous upholstery-bug, Amanda sprang out of her seat to busy herself at the kitchen sink. "Nothing," she said, as she rinsed her coffee cup. "He's probably just anxious to see you. Anyway, I'd better get my butt in gear. I've got to get to the office, make sure it's still in one piece." And she was gone.

Must have made an unusually potent pot of coffee, I thought to myself. I felt energized from head to toe. A little too energized. *Nervous energy,* I decided. After all, my boyfriend was on his way home and I hadn't seen him for over two weeks.

I headed back down the stairs for an aerobic workout. What better way to rid oneself of excess energy?! *Or so I thought...* Twenty minutes in and my heart rate had hardly budged. I changed the CD and began dancing around, losing myself in the beat of the music. After some time, Tracey, who was Chase and Amanda's cousin, appeared at the bottom of the staircase. "Come dance with me!" I shouted across the room.

Tracey wandered over and sat on the sofa. I softened the music and sat next to her.

"How was Mexico?" I heard her say. And here I thought she'd never ask!

"The pirate ship thing was *incredibly* fun. They had eye-patches and swords and everything! Wait 'til you see the pictures! We went snorkeling and there were blue fish and green fish and red fish and Amanda almost drowned! It was so funny! I don't mean funny that she almost drowned... I mean... Well, you know what I mean! Never mind. You know that expression 'You had to be there'? Well this is one of those times. Oh! Oh! I almost forgot! There was this really old lady and she was dressed all in black. She was so tall you wouldn't believe it and she talked about Jesus. She was in

Vancouver though, not in Mexico. Spanish people are so hospitable. All of them were nice and the iguanas are huge! We went to this nightclub and—"

"Joan! Joan! Slow down! I can't keep up!" Tracey interjected. She laughed at me. "You're like a TV with built-in channel surfing!"

Amanda returned from the office and the two of us ventured out to get some groceries. Chase was still a good four hours away so we'd be back in plenty of time.

Before returning home, however, we found ourselves in Amanda's favorite jewelry store. Monte, the owner, was rather fond of Amanda after years of dedicated patronage, so he immediately made it his mission to present her with an array of tempting deals.

As I browsed about, I came across the most exquisite ring I had ever seen. I simply had to have it.

After recently perfecting the art of bartering, it took but a moment to get Monte down from an obscene six thousand dollars to a respectable fifty-five hundred. I flirted shamelessly, hoping to get him to knock off another hundred or two.

The man was entirely gracious not to burst into laughter when I finally admitted I had a whopping twenty dollars for a down payment.

When we returned to the house, Tracey was waiting for us. She helped unload and put away the groceries before inviting me to her place. She lived with her sister, Erika, in an apartment across town.

Tracey was a charismatic girl with whom I'd chummed

around during my teen years. She was my best friend and a whole lot of fun, always happy and joking around, the life of every party. When it was just the two of us though, I would sometimes watch in sad wonder as that happy-go-lucky exterior of hers would fall away to expose a much shyer, insecure girl. Tracey was overweight, probably bordering on obese. A mouthful of crooked teeth also bothered her. Although I was acquainted with those parts of my friend, it would still catch me by surprise, as she'd suddenly grow sullen and withdrawn to reflect on her shortcomings. Somehow it was easy for me to overlook her weight issues, to get so lost in the laughter and sidetracked by her amazing artistic talents (she could draw like nobody's business!) that there was simply no time left to think about her being heavy. And while she was laughing, I saw only her smile and personality, not her crooked teeth.

Chase lived in Calgary during that period of time, attending the University as a student of Geology. Every summer break without fail he had shown up in our little hometown of Kimberley. 'Perfect getaway from the rat race,' he'd say.

Chase and I spent countless hours together, laughing and flirting beneath the summer sky as we fished and water-skied and went dirt biking... all under the watchful eye of his chaperoning cousins, of course. I was, after all, just eleven when my crush began. With Chase being seven years my senior, not to mention intimidated by my father, he did not reciprocate my feelings until I turned sixteen. He then became my fantasy come true, the older guy from the big city come to save a small town girl from a life destined for boredom. I was so proud to have Chase accompany me to my prom and graduation ceremony—two romantic rendezvous that would ultimately blossom into an eight-year relationship, albeit one filled with extreme highs and lows; he loves me... He loves me not... He loves me... He loves me not... *until all the petals were gone...*

By the time I learned of Chase's dark side, it was too late. I was trapped in the big city with my no-longer-so-charming Prince and my pride, too embarrassed to scurry back home to Mom and Dad.

Tracey and Erika were held captive by my lengthy narrative. I dragged them (kicking and screaming) through my entire island adventure. Together we swam and snorkeled and climbed pyramids. We drank Tequila and chased Iguanas. We met a handsome Spanish boy and some not-so-handsome pirates. We ate succulent seafood, drank a tad more Tequila, and then, in a drunken stupor... abruptly returned to the apartment to answer the telephone.

A pushing match broke out as Erika and Tracey scrambled to get to the phone first.

From clear across the room I could hear Chase's panicked voice coming through the telephone receiver. "The wind ripped the boat and trailer off the truck! We're trying to get them out of the ditch... Where the hell is everyone? We called for help an hour ago... Tell Joan I'll be there as soon as I can..."

Erika and Tracey paced the floor while I, the eternal optimist, made every attempt to reassure them. Ignoring me completely, they broke into prayer, pleading with God to get their cousin home in one piece.

Bill Smith. . . Elm Street Green

Tracey and I returned to Amanda's house to wait for Chase. So far, the relentless storm had extended his usual six-hour return trip by a good three hours.

When my boyfriend finally arrived, he appeared disheveled and exhausted. I met him at the door wearing the angelic white, off-the-shoulder dress I'd purchased in Mexico. Wrapping my arms around him, I squeezed with all my might before pulling away to twirl about before him. "Do I look like an angel?!" I shouted breathlessly, spinning 'round and 'round and 'round, white cotton billowing in all directions. Had I possessed not only *divine* qualities, but ESP as well, I likely would have heard him reply, "I'm not really sure, dear... *Are cuckoo birds white?*"

"Tell me more about your trip," Chase invited, taking my hand to lead me to the basement staircase. I knew he wanted to hear more about Lewy. He'd always had a jealous streak. But for the first time, I wasn't afraid.

We entered the bedroom where my boyfriend collapsed face-first onto the bed. I sat at the edge, too wound up to lie next to him. Not needing a second invitation, I jumped into yet another endless account of my island vacation. I held back very little, surprised by Chase's show of indifference when I again mentioned my amazing dance partner. Then, as quickly as the words came, I grew weary of talking and wandered out to the living room. There, I popped my favorite CD into the player and began bopping to the fast-paced beat of Alanna Miles.

Before long, Chase materialized in the bedroom doorway. He stood there watching me for several minutes, before taking a step in my direction. I remember thinking *this is it, the Lewy part is finally sinking in...* I stopped dancing and awaited my fate.

Casually, he strolled right past me, stopping only when he'd reached the bookshelf. I watched as he ran a fingertip over the spines of the books, caressing them thoughtfully, eyes gently leaping from title to title, as though searching for one in particular. A moment later, he extracted it from its hiding place.

Chase wandered over to the sofa where he began flipping through the pages of the textbook he'd so carefully selected. Curiosity piqued, I turned the music down and sat next to him. My boyfriend had selected psychology as one of his electives at the U of C, and now had the course book open in his lap. He found the desired chapter and, transferring the open book to my lap, said casually, "Here, hun, read this. You might find it interesting." I was so surprised at his gentle demeanor.

I began to read about a mental disorder, finding it strangely familiar at first, until it grew offensive... *intrusive* almost. It was as though the author had somehow been privy to my recent thoughts and feelings and behaviors and had taken it upon himself to tattle to the entire blinking world. Or at least everyone taking Psych 101 ...

I sensed Chase watching me. I turned to meet his gaze

and our eyes met and then he was asking if I recognized myself in what I was reading. As my eyes fell back to the pages I was surprised to hear myself admitting that yes, I most certainly did. My fingertips caressed some of the words, and then, before panic could stifle my every vocal cord, I asked... if something was wrong with me. Chase told me he wasn't sure, but not to worry, that everything would be all right.

I spent the remainder of the evening talking the ear off anyone willing to listen to my stories of Cancun. I was far from finished when everyone retired for the night so I began telephoning friends. Of course, I humbly apologized for the ungodly hour, atoning for each late night call with none other than a delightful bedtime story.

My parents and sister arrived the following day, bringing with them a most affectionate embrace. A hug from my sister anywhere anytime would be suspect enough, but what really raised the red flag were the ensuing pats on my back. Without hesitation I returned the gesture, only I was honest enough to relay the sentiment right out loud. "Ohhhh... There-there now," I said, rubbing and patting Amy Jo's back with exaggerated tenderness.

Their arrival had come as a surprise to me, as I could not recall having invited them. It was odd, too, for my parents to be skipping town in the middle of a workweek. Before I could ask too many questions, however, Chase and my parents disappeared from the room. Naturally, I began to entertain my younger sister with a story.

I believe I was in mid-stride chasing down a most agile green Iguana when the three stooges reappeared. Their mood seemed grave almost, dismal at best, which I found extremely irritating. *My goodness, people... snap out of it! What could possibly be so wrong?* (Surely nothing that a trip to Cancun couldn't cure!)

Next thing I knew, a group discussion was underway, with me the topic of conversation... Each took a turn expressing concern that I might be undergoing some sort of "episode," and suggesting it was in my best interest to see a doctor. I tossed my head back to let out a great laugh. It came out sounding more like a hyena with a sore place, really —which only annoyed me further—but I kept on smiling and said, "Gee guys, don't you think that's a little extreme? I'm happy from all the fun I had in Mexico. I feel great! Is that a crime or something?"

"You're acting weird," my sister stated, in that matter-of-fact voice that had always irked me so.

"Oh, and *you*, I suppose, are the epitome of normalcy!" I shot back. Nobody laughed, except for me. *Again, hyena... sore place...*

My parents and boyfriend spent the next while trying to persuade me to go to the hospital. They reassured me that there was, in all likelihood, not a gosh-darned thing wrong with me, just as I'd said, but to please humor them anyway. The more they droned on, the more my anxieties subsided. And then they were completely gone—my happy, carefree mood back in full force.

Imagining what an exciting adventure it might be to have my head examined, off we went to the Holy Cross Hospital. I even invited Tracey to come along for some fun.

I was pleasantly surprised at the onset to be challenged to a round of games. The handsome doctor began by calling out a set of ten, non-sequential digits. He then challenged me to repeat them, in the same order, of course.

No problem.

That was a breeze. He then repeated the exercise, rearranging the numbers while adding an additional three. I felt confident that I had once again scored perfectly. His flirtatious smile confirmed it.

Jumping into game two, DD (the dashing doctor) began by telling me to remember the phrase, "Bill Smith... Elm Street Green." He moved rapidly from there, informing me that each and every detail of the story he was about to read was vitally important, and that I must concentrate on each and every word without fail. I acknowledged the good doctor's instruction with a flirty little smile of my own.

He spouted off a very long and complicated story containing a whole host of colorful characters performing a whole host of colorful activities. Of course, I followed along as best I could, paying attention to each and every word so as not to disappoint my new suitor. Then—just when I thought the story would never end—it did.

DD began a series of questions. That, too, seemed to take forever, but eventually, forever came. *Or so I thought...*

After a brief pause, the doctor got up from his chair, crossed his arms before his chest, and challenged me to recall the initial phrase he'd told me to remember. I must say, I did not appreciate the sudden smugness in the man's tone. Suddenly Mr. Charming wasn't so charming anymore. *Perhaps a third game was in order...*

"Initial phrase?" I repeated, utter bewilderment lacing

my every syllable.

"Yes, Joan," he replied tersely. "The *initial phrase. The original grouping of words.* The two independent sentences preceding the latter multitude of co-dependent sentences intermingling within the story to become *The Story.*"

Oh, how I wanted to kick his pompous ass!

Instead, I looked to the floor, my expression pained and desperate no doubt, as tile-by-tile I searched for that all-important "initial phrase," that ever-elusive "original grouping of words"...

Without looking up, I could see the doctor's smirk clear across the room. I decided to leave him be, allow him to bask in his glory for a time...

Then, at what felt like precisely the right moment, I blurted out:

"Bill Smith! ... Elm Street Green!"

As though magically transported from his face to mine, I felt that same silly smirk at my lips. And it only broadened moments later as I watched the doctor collect his pride from the floor and scurry on out the door as though Bill Smith had set his arse on fire.

A second doctor entered the room. He was considerably older, appearing to be in his late fifties or early sixties. His smile reminded me of a really bad ad for dentures but he was courteous enough so I decided to take it easy on him. I remained on guard, however—a shrink is a shrink is a shrink.

Sporting a pair of wire-rimmed eyeglasses housing an unusually thick set of lenses, his eyes appeared to be in a perpetual state of leaping out from their sockets. Rather unnerving for the paranoid schizophrenic, I'd imagine... Hand the poor bastard a pair of 3-D glasses and it'd be all over but the rubber room!

The doctor conducted an excruciatingly boring interview, asking invasive questions about my eating and sleeping habits, my energy levels and sex drive, and if I could stand on my head, spin like a top, and recite the alphabet in reverse order.

My instincts were right. The new doctor turned out to be your stereotypical shrink, probing my brain as though it were lying in a large petri dish with his name on it. Tortured more than his fair share of rats, no doubt...

I'm not exactly sure why, but somewhere along the way I decided to share with the rodent abuser a secret I'd been keeping for some time...

I told him about a guy I knew who had two personalities. One was gentle and intelligent and liked to go on fishing trips with his friends, while the other liked to be mean and hurtful and spit on his girlfriend. I told him about how the Mean One pushed me down onto the street in broad daylight and how all the people doing yard work tried to pretend it wasn't happening.

The doctor listened so intently that I continued on, telling of how I finally made it to the Mac's convenience store —where I arrived an utter mess, sobbing uncontrollably—and how the Mean One came in immediately after me. I told how he ever so calmly came to stand alongside me, asking me ever so gently: Why are you crying? What's the matter?

And then I spoke of the brave Store Clerk... how small but mighty she was, hollering at the Mean One as though she were six feet tall instead of five-nothing. Her tenacity calmed my crying, I told the doctor, a reflective quietness in my voice now, and I was, at long last, able to call the police.

Finally, I shared with the shrink how the Police Officers strongly advised me to press charges—that in their opinion, my boyfriend was a very dangerous individual who would likely do some permanent damage given any more opportunity.

The doctor appeared sympathetic, and then disappointed moments later, when I confirmed that yes it was indeed the same boyfriend now sitting in the waiting room.

The moment I finished, the doctor again started in with the questions. I quickly grew restless, my foot tap...tap...tapping the Morse code into the flooring. But no one came to save me. I could feel my sanity slipping away. At least I was in the right place...

"Just how long is all this going to take, Doctor? I have things to do, you know."

"What kind of things?" the man with the protruding eyeballs asked.

"Important things!" I snapped, folding my arms defiantly across my chest.

"Well, okay then, Joan. Why don't you tell me about your trip to Mexico and we'll call it a day." Finally! Something worth talking about!

Before I was halfway finished, I caught the doctor glancing at his wristwatch. This made me feel anxious, not to mention annoyed as all hell, so I began to speak faster (of course), desperately trying to get in at least some of the good parts before the inevitable...

"Thank you for sharing your story." And there it was. He looked exhausted. Had he not so rudely interrupted, I might have felt sorry for him.

The doctor invited me to return to the waiting room

while he had a word with my parents. It wasn't long before he poked his head around the corner and asked Chase to join them.

Deciding to put my energies to use, I took on the challenge of livening up the waiting room with a captivating account of—you guessed it—my magical island adventure! I stood before my audience, better able to perform the more theatrical features of the story such as swimming and Iguana-chasing.

Amy and Tracey appeared spellbound. I even caught them nudging one another from time to time to exchange a WOW glance. Their veneration got me only more fired up, limbering my mind and body for the upcoming limbo competition.

"How low can you go?" I challenged, as I slid my torso beneath the imaginary bar. "Come up here, Amy Jo!" I shouted. "Everyone, this is my sister. Oh, don't be shy, Sis. Come up and show us what you've got!"

Reluctantly, my sister rose from her seat to make her way to the front of the room. She stood next to me. Everyone's eyes were upon her. She smiled nervously, whispering something I could not quite decipher. She repeated it a second time, but I remained none the wiser. She then took a deep breath, and, clear as day, and loud enough for the entire hospital to hear, said, "Snap out of it, you big freak!"

Just then, the psychiatrist appeared in the doorway. He beckoned me back to the interrogation room. "Keep my story alive," I whispered to my sister.

I followed the doctor only to be greeted with the strangest looks from my boyfriend and parents. Chase gazed at me with a look I could not for the life of me interpret; my father's face had never looked so somber; and my poor mother took but a single glimpse of me and burst into tears. I just stood there looking back at them, wondering what on earth all the fuss was about.

The doctor explained that I was undergoing an episode of mania, the first phase of a bipolar disorder called "Manic Depression." He went on to explain that Manic Depression is an illness caused by a chemical imbalance in the brain which triggers the onset of mania, also known as euphoria or elation, and after an indeterminate period of time, will end in a bout of depression. If the mania is not quickly brought under control, he warned, it could escalate into a more serious psychotic state before ever reaching the more subdued depression phase. The doctor suggested a possible culprit to be my recent consumption of Tequila. He advised me to avoid all drugs in the future, cocaine in particular, and to consume alcohol only in extreme moderation. Tequila was entirely taboo, of course. I was pleased to hear him then say that an official diagnosis of the illness could not be confirmed until a patient had experienced at least two episodes. My glimmer of hope, however, was cruelly snuffed out but a moment later when he added something to the effect that, it would, unfortunately, take "some kind of miracle" for that second episode not to come to pass...

The doctor then informed me that, after careful consideration, he, my parents and my boyfriend had come to the unanimous conclusion that it would be in my best interest to stay at the hospital's treatment facility for further observation. *One Flew Over The Cuckoo's Nest* sprang to mind, and before I knew it, I was halfway to the door, pausing only long enough to snatch away the car keys from Chase's unsuspecting hand.

I ran like the wind I did, but not so much that I couldn't relish the look of bewilderment on Nurse Ratched's face as I whizzed on by!

I found the car in the hospital parking lot and unlocked the driver's side door. Sliding onto the seat, I began fumbling for the ignition key. Even though I did not have a driver's license, I was fully prepared to take flight.

As I tried the first key, I suddenly realized that I hadn't locked the door. I pressed the switch to the "lock" position—and not a moment too soon. Tracey peered at me through the passenger side window as she tried unsuccessfully to open the door. I stuck my tongue out at her and continued my search for the ignition key. She appeared beside me, rapping at the window.

I ignored her.

She rapped harder.

I jammed the final key into the ignition and started the car.

"Ple-e-e-ease!" Tracey hollered.

I revved the engine.

"Joan! Come on! Talk to me!" she pleaded. I pressed the power button and lowered the window a touch. "Don't be crazy! Oops... Sorry, Joan. I didn't mean that. Just let me in, okay? You know me. I'm on your side. I promise."

"Go around to the other side," I said, unlocking the doors.

Tracey slid in next to me. "Listen carefully...we don't have much time...they're figuring out a plan as we speak."

The girl was babbling so fast that I had to wonder if mania was contagious. "I overheard them talking," she continued, nearly out of breath. "I know what you've gotta do,

Joan. If a person is a danger to their own self or to another person they can be institutionalized *against* their will. It's time for your acting debut. You're going to have to convince them that you're sane enough to be out and about. Fleeing in a vehicle without a driver's license probably won't help your case and—"

"I'm not crazy," I interjected. "And I won't be carted off to some nutbar hotel without a fight. Do you know what goes on in those places?!" When I turned to Tracey, she appeared deep in thought.

"You trust me, don't you?" she asked after a time.

"Uhh... Yeah..."

"Well, here's the thing. They're going to come looking for you any minute. You've got to go in before they come out. You need to apologize... say you're sorry... that you got scared. I'll come with you. And no matter what, you have to keep your cool. If you do, I promise they can't make you stay unless you want to."

"Are you sure?"

"Positive. But we have to go now or it'll be too late." Tracey glanced over at the hospital doors. I followed suit. No sign of Nurse Ratched... *yet.*

"This had better not be a trick," I said, as I reached tentatively for the door handle.

I was awarded freedom for my performance. Upon hearing the wonderful news, I also found out that I was to receive from the doctor a tiny, blue pill. It was, without doubt, the smallest pill I had ever seen. Not only did it look like the offspring of a saccharine tablet, but also, came with a guarantee that I would feel like my old self in "no time at all." Although I'd grown rather fond of the new me, the tiny pill appeared harmless enough... so, I swallowed it.

Before we were halfway home, my mind was completely fogged over. I could barely form a complete thought. The only thing I knew for certain was that I wanted to cry. But the tears wouldn't come. As the car rounded each corner, my head lolled forward as though my neck was broken, bobbing this way and that way like some crazy bobble-head doll. I tried using my hands to hold it upright, but even that proved difficult.

Soon, my entire body was without motor function. It was as though my brain had somehow disconnected from the rest of me and I'd turned into little more than a rag doll. My arms grew heavy and fell to my sides. My head remained upright for one hopeful moment, a basketball in the balance deciding whether or not to drop through the hoop... And then it did. As my chin came to rest on my chest once again, the remainder of my body slid lower into the seat. And then lower...

It felt as though every muscle and bone had vacated my body and at any moment I might slither to the floor to become a lifeless pile of pink flesh with two eyeballs peeking out the top.

Chase carried my limp body into the house and down the basement stairs where he gently placed me on the bed. He later told me that I'd remained so perfectly motionless that he'd checked frequently through the night to make sure I was even breathing. He also told me how the doctor had tried to convince him to leave me, telling him that I would always be a burden and he'd be much better off without me. Chase assured me that that would never happen, that he would never, ever, EVER leave me.

At first I thought, *what a heartless bastard of a doctor!*
And then I thought, *or is he...?*

Pricilla & the Ray-ban Man

I awoke to a fit of shivering. The bedding beneath me was damp with perspiration, my body on fire, yet my teeth would not stop chattering. For nearly twelve hours I'd been in a coma-like state, yet I felt exhausted beyond belief. Nothing made sense.

My happy high was gone, that much was certain. No more happy mania. Sometime during the night a cruel depression had taken over, and if it weren't for an urgent need to relieve myself, I likely would have surrendered to it and stayed in bed another twelve hours. I couldn't remember ever feeling so tired. Every inch of my body felt heavy, my spirit crushed beneath the weight of it all. It was an effort just to breathe.

I managed to get out of bed but by the time I located my housecoat, I was ready to crawl back in. If there'd only been a suitable container lying around...

The fullness of my bladder grew to a persistent ache. It was the only thing that kept me moving. The basement was not entirely self-contained, and as I stepped foot onto the staircase leading to the main-floor bathroom, I was reminded of the steep pyramids we'd recently climbed. Only this time, there was no surge of energy to boost me onto that first step.

Everything was a challenge, from bathing to dressing to putting on makeup. (Amazing how vanity becomes so ingrained in a girl's psyche; really and truly, could anyone have cared less if I went without makeup for a day? But somehow it seemed important so I got the job done. Perhaps, deep down, I was hoping that in *looking* better, I might somehow *feel* better.)

Eating was another challenge. Not so much the act of raising food to my mouth, but rather, having to force myself to chew and swallow once it arrived. Blessed with a more than efficient metabolism, I had always taken full advantage, but now food had lost its appeal.

Chase and my parents accompanied me to the hospital for my follow-up visit with the doctors. The debilitating effects of the medication had almost completely worn off at this point, but the depression was worsening. I felt sad and hopeless. I felt painfully lonely, even when surrounded by family and friends.

After a dozen or so questions, the doctors prescribed a mood-stabilizer called Lithium. They also recommended I be admitted to the psychiatric ward until my depression could be brought under control. Again, I became agitated with the idea, but my parents and boyfriend persisted, convincing me it was for my own good. Too tired to argue, I relented.

As I was being led to my room, which would turn out to be halfway down the west wing of the hospital's psych ward, I passed by a number of patients. Their eyes appeared vacant, haunted almost, and mouths droopy, as though they hadn't smiled in a very long time.

It was an obese fellow with a friendly, brown face who accompanied me to my new quarters. I liked him immediately.

And then I noticed his incredibly large Colgate smile. It seemed almost out of place. *Is he mocking everyone?* I wondered. But as he proceeded to flash his pearly whites and call out to each patient by name, I knew he was the real deal. I especially liked that he did not treat me as a "crazy" person. I let my guard down further.

The room was simple, containing a small cot with over-starched linen, a lumpy pillow attempting to hide in its casing, also over-starched, and a small, wooden table with matching chair. The table and chair sat below a solitary window, which was clad in a set of the busiest curtains I had ever seen. They looked so out of place in the otherwise drab room. And then I figured it out. The hodgepodge of color and activity served as camouflage; and it almost certainly would have worked, had it not been for the slight part in the center. There, peeking out at me from within... a tall silver... I narrowed my eyes to get a second opinion...

Sure enough! *My window had bars!* Had I not felt so completely and utterly blah, I might well have given a damn.

Atop the table sat a piece of paper accompanied by a ballpoint pen. The large man with the perpetual smile pulled the chair out from beneath the table and invited me to sit. Then, with dimples burrowing ever deeper into his pleasantly plump cheeks, he said, "Go ahead, now. Read that over. Signature at the bottom. Make yourself at home, Sweetie. It's really not such a bad place. I promise." He winked, and left me alone.

Halfheartedly, I skimmed over the consent form and signed my life away, officially becoming Holy Cross Hospital's frowny-faced inmate number ninety-nine.

I wandered back up the hallway and found Chase in the

dining area. "I don't like it here," I told him simply.

"Don't worry," he replied. "You won't have to stay long. Everything's gonna be okay. You'll see. I'll be here with you as much as I can, and I'll bring you some books to read."

"Yeah... Make sure you bring *One Flew Over the—*"

Without warning, the woman seated at the table next to us began shouting at the top of her lungs:

"Do I look like a whore?! Do I look like a whore?! Do I look like a whore?!"

She just kept saying it, over and over and over, as though she might never stop.

"Ohhh...myyy...gawwwd!" I whispered to Chase, not that there was much danger of anyone else hearing me.

Although the woman with the lungs was still going strong, my attention was soon diverted to a young man seated several tables away. He appeared to be in his mid-twenties and might even have passed for "normal" if not for the oversized mirrored sunglasses eclipsing half his face.

I watched as he slowly, methodically removed the rind from the orange in his hand to separate the naked fruit into two, equal halves. Then, tearing off a single segment from one of the halves, he proceeded to make a partial tear in its center. Slowly, he raised the segment of orange to his mouth, holding it between the tips of forefinger and thumb, forefinger and thumb, a pair at either end, to gently pry it apart at its torn center. He held it there a moment, and then, just as the moment began to linger, his lips started to part. My forehead furrowed slightly when he made no effort to put the orange in his mouth... And surely my eyebrows leapt clean up to my hairline a second later when the guy's tongue came slithering out! And then... well... let's just say it became apparent in a hurry that Mr. Ray-ban Man indeed had a crush on his little piece of fruit...

I felt almost violated. I just knew that somewhere beyond those ridiculously large sunglasses there was, all the while, a pervy pair of eyeballs boring a hole through my clothing. I'd never seen anyone perform oral sex on an orange before (or any other type of fruit for that matter), but once was enough to know that it just wasn't right. And with Pricilla the Prostitute still going strong, it was more than I could bear.

"I'm outta here!" I whispered to Chase. Then, as casually as I could, I stood up and headed for my room.

No sooner had I placed one foot in front of the other did I notice the big burly intern watching from across the room. He was *not* smiling. Our eyes met, and then, horror of all horrors, he began a beeline towards the west wing.

And the race was on!

Somehow my tired body had rejuvenated itself, producing enough adrenaline to propel my feet, and in no time, I'd outdistanced the fat man by a pretty good margin. I arrived at my room with time to spare, obliterating my signature with a hundred-and-one strokes of ink.

Like darling little butterflies the last few pieces of shredded consent form fluttered gracefully to the floor, just as Beefcake Boy darkened the doorway. He stood there staring at me, his large barrel chest heaving in and out as he struggled to catch his breath. I waited for angina to strike, for him to clutch his chest and topple over like a large building having been struck by a wrecking-ball. But he remained upright, and as his breathing slowed I couldn't help but smile a little victory smile. He wagged a thick, meaty finger at me, but all I really noticed was that signature smile twitching there at the corners of his lips.

"Anything I can say to change your mind, Missy?"

"Nope. Thanks. Pricilla said it all. Oh, and the guy with the fruit-fetish... He did his fair share of tongue wagging, too... *if ya catch my drift*."

"I'm sorry you had to witness that. Truly I am. But it isn't always like that..."

"Look Mister, I appreciate what you're trying to do here, but I feel like crap and I just want to go home." And with that, I excused myself and headed off to find Chase.

Assuming the sliding glass doors would open automatically, I nearly ran headfirst into them before realizing permission to exit was required—I guess they'd decided it best Pricilla and the fruit guy not come and go at will. Escape would not be so easily realized for me either, however.

The attendant paged the bug-eyed doctor.

A wave of fear washed over me. I stood there, my mind reeling, terrified that at any moment I would be stuck with a needle and carted off for a session of shock therapy. Or perhaps a simple lobotomy would be in order. I squeezed my eyes shut and began to pray, silently pleading with God to spare me from such a fate...

With little attempt to persuade me otherwise, the good doctor granted me permission to leave the ward. He asked me to accompany him to the other side of the hospital for a brief discussion, promising to let me go immediately afterwards.

Turned out he was indeed a very caring doctor, displaying genuine concern for my welfare. When asked if I'd be willing to visit a colleague-slash-friend of his for a few follow-up sessions, I agreed. I did refuse, however, to start the Lithium program. Whatever the heck that little blue pill was that brought me crashing down from my happy high, if it were any indication of what was to come, then no thanks!

The kind doctor shook my hand and wished me well.

I deeply inhaled the fresh, glorious air that was my freedom, too exhausted to do anything but breathe and thank God for getting me out of that hellhole.

10

Has a Nice Ring to It

Was it my faithful abstinence from drinking Tequila? The power of prayer, perhaps? Or was it that "some kind of miracle" to which the doctor had referred? The new Millennium marked for me a twelve-year anniversary with sanity. Well, perhaps that is a bit of a stretch... Can't say I've ever been accused of being an *entirely* sane person. Oh, well... point being, I've never experienced a second episode of Manic Depression, while remaining one hundred percent medication-free.

It took the better part of eight long years to realize that Chase and I were not soul mates after all—a few too many bruises, both inside and out, perhaps being the largest clue ...

About a year prior to my breakup with Chase, I had secured a job as a Commercial Lending Secretary at a bank in downtown Calgary. There, I developed a close friendship with another secretary by the name of Janessa Reeves. Janessa took pity on me as I lamented over my failed relationship, earnestly endeavoring to cheer me up. So off to the nightclub we went, to that magical place where troubles are checked at the door, and where one's every woe is put on hold allowing the carefree atmosphere of music and booze, bumping and grinding, to become a temporary pain reliever for everything that ails them.

My friend and I were attempting to converse over the impossibly loud music when I noticed a guy gazing at me. He was tall, I figured about six feet or so, had dark wavy hair and a moustache. The immediate flutter of butterfly wings suggested the possibility of love at first sight—or at least the potential for some bumping and grinding on the dance floor...

The butterflies fluttered out of control as he approached, and only grew more restless as I noticed his full lips. They appeared pillow-soft and when they parted I was surprised, pleasantly, by the soft-spoken manner with which they addressed me. "Would you care to dance?" my handsome stranger asked. I couldn't help but notice that as he spoke, his eyes left mine to peer at the floor. I perceived his shyness as charming, rather than a lack of confidence. It was refreshing to meet a more subdued ego, especially one wrapped in such attractive packaging.

We talked and danced and he drank, and although we didn't do much bumping and grinding, a positive enough connection was established for me to offer the man my telephone number.

As Adam and I explored each other's eyes over lunch, I was delighted to discover that he looked every bit as handsome in the daylight as he had under the hypnotic spell of night. I was pleased also that his charm remained intact, as I had feared that it might have evaporated along with the alcohol on his breath.

After learning that Adam's charm and good looks were

accompanied also by a most pleasant personality, I invited him back to my apartment. As we passed by the answering machine I casually pressed the play button to retrieve the waiting messages.

We found the much-too-soft couch, and a moment later, were seated side-by-side like a set of conjoined twins after sinking in unison into its marshmallow center. Neither of us seemed to mind however, as we surrendered to the moment, all twitterpated and smiling shyly at one another. And then we were completely lost, eyes twinkling with delight, enjoying the sensation of our shared body warmth... drunk in the euphoria of that fresh, new romance... where no one else existed...

...except that dang voice penetrating our reverie, "Hi Joan! It's your sister calling! I just got your message about your new boyfriend! You sound so excited and I'm so happy for you! He sounds cute and nice, and who knows, maybe he's even the one! I can't wait to meet—"

By the time I reached the answering machine, the entire cat was out of the bag. Stupid couch! (... not exactly easy to get up when your rear-end has sunk so far down between the cushions that your own knobby knees are serving as a chin rest). Adam was gracious enough to give me a good hard shove in the end (literally!), but it was too little, too late.

As it turned out, he was entirely taken with my sister's barrage of compliments—enough to last a lifetime, no doubt.

We gazed intently at the television screen, although neither of us were aware of what may have been transpiring there. Occasionally, I glanced out through the clear glass patio doors that opened onto the grassy grounds of the apartment complex. Soon, I caught sight of a cute little dog roaming about, crossing out signatures to create new ones of his own. He was fluffy and white and I must say, appeared to possess a remarkably large inkwell for such a small dog.

As he neared the patio doors to claim a particular shrub he thought he might like to own, I crept over to slide the doors open. Then, after lowering myself to all fours, I began coaxing him to me. Concerned that he might be lost, I wanted to check for a collar and tags.

And then there he was... the dog's master... just a short distance away, leash dangling idly from one hand.

"Oh my gawd... I see his owner," I whispered to Adam, backing away from the door. Fearing the stranger might think I was trying to nab his precious bundle of fur, I hoped to disappear before he had a chance to spot me.

I sank into the sofa, nestling in comfortably next to my handsome, new boyfriend. I felt his eyes on me... Slowly, I turned to meet his longing gaze... It would be our very first kiss...

Oh, the butterflies!

But there were no puckered lips to be had. Instead, I was met by a peculiar half-smile accompanied by a most inquisitive pair of brown eyes.

"Why are you looking at me like that?" I asked, feeling vulnerable and shy suddenly, not to mention ridiculous.

"I don't know," he replied. I could see that he was trying not to laugh. My cheeks began to burn, as every last butterfly vanished without a trace.

"You don't know?" I said, my voice rising an octave or two. "Come on, Adam. I think you do."

"Well...alright... I guess I'm just a little surprised by what you said. You know, seeing how we just met."

Completely at a loss, I replied, "What exactly is it that you think I said?"

"Did you not say, 'Oh my gawd, I see his boner!'?"

We shared many more laughs over the next nine months, spending every possible minute together. Adam attended college, and was on the verge of finishing up his studies to become an Electronic Technician. He so enjoyed my company that he held his every study session at my apartment.

We playfully argued about which one of us was sexier. Adam would start off with "You're sexy," to which I'd immediately counter with "Thanks! But you're sexier!" Finally, and with great triumph, he would announce, "And you're the SEXIEST!" It was no surprise when his pet name for me became "Sexy," and although it made me feel both flattered and oh so desirable, he became so accustomed to addressing me as such that he often did so in public. I suppose there were worse things he could have called me. Still, I couldn't help but feel a slight twinge of embarrassment. Combined with my father's nickname for me, I'd become a real Sexy Chick!

I was surprised at how nervous Adam seemed about meeting my folks. He was restless and fidgety and when the doorbell sounded, he downed the last of his beer so fast I thought he would choke on it.

Shortly after introductions were made my sister beckoned me to the kitchen.

"He's really cute!" she exclaimed.

"I know! I really like him! I think I'm going to marry him!"

My heart grew even fonder of my beloved Adam while vacationing at Premier Lake. It was there that he displayed for me not only a most impressive feat of strength, but also, chivalry, the old-fashioned kind, that once-upon-a-time foreplay guaranteed to knock your knickers off. This day, however, there would be no knickers. Nope. Not-a-one. There was, however, this one itsy bitsy teensy weensy yellow polka dot...

We were in the midst of inflating our rubber dinghy when Adam noticed a young woman in the water, struggling to pull herself onto the wharf. Off strode my brave knight to rescue the damsel in distress.

Standing on the pier overlooking the woman, Adam graciously offered his hand to her. She accepted, placing her delicate hand within his strong one. With the greatest of ease Adam began to pull the young woman from the water. Every muscle in his arm rippled, his tanned six-pack (of beer) gleaming in the sunlight. And then something went awry... *terribly* awry. Horror of all horrors, he'd yanked her too hard, nearly sending her cartwheeling over his head to land in the water on the other side of the dock! And to make matters worse, the woman had been torn from the water with such tremendous force that her strapless bathing suit top had rolled down to cover her bellybutton. Adam's face turned three shades of red as he glimpsed the woman's bare breasts flapping in the wind before him, and then his eyes were at her feet.

I found myself thinking of the night Adam and I met... of that shy invitation to join him on the dance floor, uttered with such uncertainty as he peered down at my feet. But something told me that if he uttered that same invitation now—in that exact same charming manner—still, it was doubtful that the half-naked damsel on the dock would break out into a whole lot of pirouetting anytime soon!

And then there was my own cunning feat just a short time later...

Adrift in the tranquil waters beneath the warm afternoon sky, we were entirely at ease, fishing poles dangling leisurely over the sides of our little craft, fish apparently too lazy to bite. Adam chain-smoked one after the other from his package of Players Light, while enjoying a few cool Kokanees (not the trout kind... the beer!). I, too, puffed away on a cigarette, although mine went better with 7-Up, blowing near-perfect smoke rings through the still air while keeping careful watch on my rod.

Suddenly there came a loud hissing sound. I followed the noise to discover a hole in the dinghy... right near the tip of my cigarette! I panicked, but only momentarily before my survival instincts kicked in. Quickly, I reached into my jeans-jacket pocket to retrieve the package waiting there. Although it was hot and sweaty and half-melted by the sun, I managed to get one stick unwrapped and into my mouth. It didn't require much chewing, as it was already soft and pliable...

(I'm sure you can figure out the rest, but I will say one final thing: although Adam did not come right out and say it, I have no doubt that he was entirely blown away with his girlfriend's McGuyver-like skills.)

The day for "swapping secrets" inevitably arrived, and seeing how Adam didn't have any, I let him have mine with both barrels. *Or should I say kegs?* I told him the entire story, every sordid detail, from the keg of Tequila to the fruit-licking freak in the sunglasses. *What better way to test a boyfriend's love?*

I got quite emotional and even more so when, immediately afterward, Adam up and left the apartment with barely a word.

And then panic set in.

I began to question everything... *Did I mention I'd had only the ONE episode? Check. Did I show him enough pictures of me in my bikini? Check, check. Did I talk too much about Lewy? Uh Ohhh...*

Adam's face never looked as good as it did the moment he walked back through that door—in his hand, a bouquet of flowers, accompanied by a tiny, white envelope. The miniature note read:

These flowers I give to you
Because you seem so blue
Don't ever let it be forgot
That I love you a lot

Had I died and gone to Heaven? Not only was it an incredibly romantic gesture, but also, one of the most endearing things anyone had ever done for me. I could not have cherished the moment more. Unless, of course, I'd known just how rare such an occasion would turn out to be ...

Adam's marriage proposal was not nearly as grand as the ring that went with it, but I didn't mind. The oversized heart-shaped rock more than made up for any lack of sentiment! (To be honest, it came as no real surprise. After all, it appeared much the same as the manic day I'd chosen it...) I marveled at the familiar object now sparkling at my finger, the months of relentless persuasion having finally paid off. And although my fiancé displayed no outward sign of resentment about the hundred-and-five-year payment plan that came with it, I had a sneaking suspicion it was festering there somewhere inside.

Oh, but what a rock! Did I mention it was heart-shaped?

In the summer of '92 I married the man who'd given me the pretty ring.

The Flawless Fiancé

By 1994 our marriage was in trouble. I believe the first sign of disharmony to be the change in my pet name. My sex appeal must have worn off or something because instead of "Sexy," I'd suddenly become "Hag-bag."

Adam was a realist, and I was a great dreamer. Our personalities could not have been more opposite. For example, my philosophy on "the purpose of life":

Experience as much fun as possible while one is young and able.

Adam's went something about life being a challenge, an arena of one's endurance—a place to work as hard as possible until one is old and unable. Oh, joy...

We joked about suing the people who had put our marriage on its course. Thinking back, I remember one exercise in particular where Adam and I were to take turns revealing one another's imperfections. We each had to come up with at least two. Adam went first.

"I can't..." he finally muttered, after opening and shutting his mouth several times without so much as a sound. (I don't know that I ever told him so, but he rather reminded me of a fish out of water trying to say, "I can't... breathe.")

Just as one of the counselors was about to let him off the hook, my soon-to-be husband piped up to say, "I can't think of a thing. Seriously... she's perfect!"

The husband and wife team nearly split a gut. Even I had to laugh. Adam's face reddened, and as he shifted in his seat, for one horrifying moment I thought he was preparing to leap off the couch and attack the happy couple.

"Well... okay then. I can think of *one* thing," Adam said, when at last the laughter died down.

"Do tell, Adam," the woman urged, trying hard to stay composed. "What is your future wife's one imperfection?"

"She does too much," Adam replied.

Everyone waited for more... But nothing more came.

"She does too much what, Adam?" the woman prompted. "Are you saying Joan is a workaholic?" At this point, the woman's husband coughed into his hand, obviously attempting to stifle a laugh. That's when I felt my own hackles starting to rise. Was it really so hard to imagine that I might be capable of working too much???

"No... not exactly," Adam said slowly. "I just mean that she does too much... you know... *nice* stuff." The three of us burst into laughter. The way he'd emphasized the word "nice" had sent our minds straight into the gutter. Poor Adam turned beet red.

I rubbed my fiancé's back affectionately and thanked him for the compliment, but apparently he felt the need to clarify. "All I meant is that she likes to do things for me... you know, cooking and laundry. Stuff like that. Comprende vous, ya great big a-holes!" He didn't say the last part, but I knew he was thinking it.

By the time it was my turn, I didn't have the heart to say one bad thing about my future husband.

Our wedding was rich with Catholic tradition, although I'm not sure if it was more for Adam and me, or for our parents. I had returned to the Catholic Church shortly after Chase and I parted ways, although I'm not sure it mattered so much as to *what* church I went back to. I just wanted to grow closer to the amazing God who'd saved me from the manic depression and a possible lifetime of relationship regrets. Adam accompanied me to church for a brief time, before work began to monopolize his every spare minute.

Our honeymoon was short and sweet, and all too soon followed by the realization that married life really does suck. I'd heard it a hundred times, but I was so sure that we would be the exception.

The moment we returned from Montana, my new husband began spending more and more time working, and less and less time with me. To make matters worse, I wound up on stress leave from my job at the bank. Jigsaw puzzles kept me entertained for a while, but eventually I grew restless, and somehow our apartment became the focus of my discontent. I longed for a house to call home... And what was a home without a couple of pooches?

Once again persistence paid off, and within a year we'd purchased our first home and a pair of dogs to go with it. Unfortunately, though, it seemed the house had come with some kind of curse. Adam suddenly detested affection. He did not like to give affection... he did not like to receive affection. I spent every waking moment trying to figure out what was suddenly so wrong with me. When I'd confront Adam, he would insist it was "nothing" or that he "just didn't like to hold hands or be touched."

My sister and her husband came to stay with us while their house was being built. One night, probably a Friday or a Saturday, the four of us cozied up on the couch to watch a movie. Adam sat at one end, my brother-in-law at the other, and my sister and I side-by-side in the middle. (I practically had to extend a written invitation to get my husband to join us, as he preferred to sit alone.)

It had been a while since the two of us were "joined at the hip," so I was practically giddy about the whole thing. I felt like I was on a date! And it was even okay if my husband found out! And then something went terribly wrong. Somewhere along the way, silly, silly me went and forgot about my husband's newly acquired arachnophobia...

We must have been watching a mushy chick-flick, although I can't recall for certain, or maybe the touchy-feely couple in our midst inspired my lapse in judgement. At any rate, it was without any forethought of the consequences that I reached out and... put my hand on Adam's leg!

The next thing I know my hand is back in my own lap, and I didn't put it there!

My sister elbowed me. I looked at her. She spoke with her eyes, arching an eyebrow to look first to Adam's lap and then to mine. I gave her the "Shhh" sign. She turned the other way to whisper to her husband.

Eventually Adam had to make a beer run, and the second he was gone, Amy Jo piped up to say, "Holy cow! He picked up your hand like it was a Tarantula and dropped it into your lap! Doesn't that hurt your feelings?" I told her that yes, it did hurt my feelings, but I'd pretty much gotten used to it.

(Years later I would come to learn the reason for Adam's

rejection. He told me that he had felt pressured to buy the house and that, in doing so, he'd been made to feel as though he'd lost control in our relationship. He said that when he withheld and rejected affection, it made him feel empowered. I wished he could have just talked to me...)

As our financial obligations grew, so, too, did the number of hours Adam worked. Perfectly logical for the realist, I suppose, although not a lot of fun for Dreamer Girl.

My search for happiness intensified.

It wasn't long before the novelty of being a homeowner had worn off, and in its place, a fantasy about owning a shiny red Stealth came to pass. Understandable, considering the fact that our little Chevy Cavalier was an utterly dull vehicle, capable of little more than the practical feat of transporting its occupants from A to B. Adam kindly offered to sell our house and buy me my dream car, just as long as I was willing to consider it our new place of residence as well. *Partypooper...*

My fantasy became somewhat of a reality a short time later. It happened as our trustworthy Cavalier was transporting me from work to home one afternoon, as I made a shoulder check to change lanes in the bumper-to-bumper rushhour traffic. It took only a moment, but when I returned my eyes to the road ahead, I was met by the ominous, red brake lights of the Audi before me.

I stomped on the brake pedal with all my might, but to no avail; my cherished Cavalier slammed full-force into the rear of the expensive import. I just sat there, stunned, staring at the buckled hood of my car. And then I wondered if I had hit my face. Reaching up, I touched my nose, my cheeks, my chin, before glancing in the rearview mirror to be certain. Then, with unsteady hands, I removed my lifesaving seatbelt and proceeded to open the door.

What a sight I must have been, standing there in the busy street, miniskirt billowing in the breeze, bright, red blood trickling down my wobbly legs from the gashes at my knees. (I've since broken the habit of sitting so close to the dashboard.)

The gentleman driver of the now demolished Audi approached to ask if I was all right, expressing concern for my mutilated legs. Tears streamed down my face as I apologized for my blunder. Moments later, a paramedic dabbed at my lacerations to gleefully announce that they appeared superficial and would not require stitching. Meanwhile, from the not too far distance, I could hear his partner making a valiant effort to convince the gentleman whose vehicle I had struck to accompany him to the hospital. As the man's whiplash worsened with each passing second, he was barely able to shake his head "no" in reply. The considerate motorist was too preoccupied with my injuries to worry about his own. He just kept saying, "Look at her knees! Look at her knees!" over and over like a broken record.

As we sat in the police car filling out the accident report, I sadly announced that it was my husband's birthday. I then proceeded to sing a few lines from the jolly ditty "Happy Birthday to You." I did so entirely out of tune, laughing and sobbing all the while. It was right about then, I believe, that one of the officers asked if I had perhaps banged my head during the crash.

Upon arriving home, I telephoned my husband to wish

him a happy birthday before announcing that I had totaled the car. The horrible incident was all but forgotten a week later, as I slid into my shiny, new, red Beretta.

It wasn't long after the car crash when my husband began to suspect that I was purposely staging "accidents" in order to realize my desires. I solemnly swore that it was an entirely unplanned event when I sat on and demolished my no-longer-fashionable eyeglasses. And it was no less coincidental when, several days after mentioning I wanted new flooring in the kitchen, I should happen to boil a pot until it melted and oozed down onto the linoleum like liquid mercury.

As it turned out however, mere renovations to our existing home didn't quite cut it for me. I longed to live in a charming log home surrounded by untamed wilderness, where my darling dogs could dash after the deer and my handsome horses could frolic freely through the open fields of green... And who knows... perhaps we'd all meet up later for a drink at the happy little stream trickling through our blessed piece of paradise.

Adam now worked seven days a week, ten to twelve hours a day. Was he, too, dreaming of that quaint little cabin at the edge of the wood? Our very own home on the range where the deer and the dogs and the horses could play? Hmmm...

The Taxman

After several years of playing the unfulfilling role of secretary, I became a caregiver, providing home support to a woman with Parkinson's. With the support of round-the-clock caregivers, Kate was fortunate enough to remain in the comfort of her own home. Her husband, John, a successful entrepreneur, provided her with a lavish home in a prestigious neighborhood along with all the niceties that go hand in hand with wealth.

I admired Kate Wellington immensely. She'd been afflicted with the cruel disease early in life, and from the onset, battled with it courageously over the years. Although she was now confined to a wheelchair, her sense of humor remained intact.

Kate enjoyed venturing out to the various bars and lounges in the city to try her luck on the VLT machines (Video Lottery Terminals, AKA Slot Machines). So when I came along, we decided to make it a part of our routine, venturing out once or twice a week in hot pursuit of "The Big Win."

In the beginning, I merely watched. Kate liked to play a game called "Five Way," and in order for her to strike it rich, she had to line up five pieces of fruit, bells or sevens into a perfect v-shape from corner to corner, or a straight line across the screen—top, center or bottom. I found myself engrossed with the game, mesmerized by the vibrantly colored cherries, oranges, plums and bells. Oh, and *Oooo La, La!... Those MAGICAL RED SEVENS!!* A perfect row of lucky sevens on a double bet landed a quick five hundred dollars. Whenever a player won two hundred or more credits (each credit valued at twenty-five cents), a bright red light atop the machine would leap into action, flashing wildly as the fresh batch of credits was tallied on the screen.

What a thrill it was to witness Kate hit her first win. She grinned from ear to ear as her red light announced her victory, and giggled like a schoolgirl as her small fortune of credits climbed to a whopping five hundred plus dollars. It was nice to see her having so much fun. Seemed almost a godsend, really—the perfect diversion from the relentless monotony of her illness.

I simply couldn't help myself. I had to give it a try. Dropping just a small number of one-dollar coins into the slot, I ventured a modest beginner's bet. Pleasant memories of my trip to Las Vegas surfaced as I got reacquainted with the slot machine. I won a little, lost a little, and had a whole lot of fun in the process.

And so it began. Rarely did I spend more than twenty dollars on any given outing, and I even managed to leave with a small profit from time to time. Gradually my bets increased, as did my wins and losses.

Before my gambling obsession began, I sincerely believe that I was a good person. Sure I had character defects: I told the occasional fib, was hopelessly addicted to nicotine, tended to be selfish and self-centered at times, and was known to be rather relentless in my general pursuit of love and happiness. Thank God I was bestowed with a multi-faceted personality (not to be confused with a multiple personality disorder), which allowed for good qualities also...

My adoptive mother shaped within me a kind and generous heart, one that allowed me to love my family and friends immensely and unconditionally. And then there was my sense of humor. This (often-misunderstood) quality could only have been bestowed me by my new father. Apparently his (ridiculously) dry sense of humor had (mercilessly) seeped into my psyche the moment we'd met... No one else in my new family possessed such a trait. My fondness for the animal kingdom also came from him. As far back as I can remember he had always displayed a most remarkable appreciation for even the "least" of God's creatures—spiders! No wonder the inevitable day arrived when I became the proud owner of a large black Tarantula! (Not to mention Envy, the green Iguana, and Twinkie, Blinkie, Tater & Boo the happy mouse family, which, by the way, inexplicably expanded to include Hilda, Hagatha, Spanky, Moo-Moo, Fruitloop, Smudge and...)

Regardless of how "multi-faceted" my personality may have been, it was about to take on characteristics far beyond anything my wildest imagination could ever have dreamed up...

It was during one of my days off when I decided to venture out on my own to try my luck at the slots. As I showered and dressed, the butterflies in my stomach began to flutter out of control, the anticipation of watching the colorful shapes line up on a VLT screen simply overwhelming.

I pulled into the parking lot of the mini strip-mall and stopped before the pub I intended to visit. But first, I would hurry into the 7-11 next door to withdraw some money from its ATM. I wasn't sure if the tiny bar would have such a thing, and did not feel like wasting time in finding out that it didn't.

A man with an embroidered bald eagle on the back of his well-worn jean jacket stood in the line before me. He smelled like a dirty ashtray and I was glad when it was his turn, although he seemed to take forever and a day to accept the fact that the machine was not going to give him one red cent. Finally, mumbling something under his breath, he turned and headed for the door.

I had better luck and with two crisp twenties in hand, entered the little pub, the tacky neon sign above its heavy wooden door so incredibly bright I was nearly rendered sightless. They must have recently changed the tubing. That, or some ambitious soul had given it its annual scrub bath.

As my eyes adjusted to the sudden dimness within, immediately I set my sights on the slot machines against the far wall. I was disappointed to discover that each was occupied. As I waited for one to become available, I spotted an elderly woman of about seventy-five walking slowly away from her machine. Out of courtesy, I approached her to confirm that she was indeed finished. An angry expression crossed her face as she snapped, "Of course I'm not finished! Don't be so stupid!" I stood there dumbfounded, my face burning with embarrassment as I watched her continue on her way to the coin dispenser.

A young fellow seated at another of the slot machines

beckoned me over. In a whisper he explained how the elderly woman was a regular, showing up at the exact same time each and every day to play the exact same machine. She never played another machine as far as he could recall. Probably had her name on it somewhere, he said. *Yeah... Broom Hilda!...* He went on to explain that "the poor thing" had been on a losing streak for about a week and was becoming more and more ornery with each passing day. Even the barmaids avoided her. I heard her voice in my head: *I may look old and decrepit, but my legs work just fine thank you very much, and if I need a drink or a lousy snack from your greasy menu I'll waltz on over and ask for it! And while we're at it... why don't you put some clothes on, young lady? Place ain't indecent enough for ya?*

It turned out that, at the time of our meeting, she'd already lost over five hundred dollars. It wasn't even noon yet. I remember feeling sorry for her and wondering why she didn't just stop...

Eventually a machine became available, and although my eyes had followed its last player until he'd disappeared through the door clearly marked with a bright neon *EXIT*, I couldn't help but glance over my shoulder a time or two from the still-warm barstool.

I placed in my lap the white Styrofoam bowl I had filled with one-dollar coins from the dispenser and inserted a handful of them into the slot. I selected the one game I was familiar with and pressed the spin button. Five purple plums lined up in a perfect row. The red light atop my machine sprang to life, flashing on and off as my credits tick-tick-tick-tick-ticked their way up to two hundred fifty. Several players congratulated me. What a fabulous feeling! And on my very first spin!

I admired my score a time before resuming play with the hope of winning even more. Five of a kind lined up three more times in near-perfect succession. Each time, I gazed up in wonder at my little red light, basking in the crimson glow of victory as though the Lord himself were shining down on me. *My exquisite, red rose...*

It was exhilarating to see over one thousand credits displayed before me on my screen. I'd seen Kate win as much and more, but never had any such luck myself. I took a moment to calculate my winnings. At two hundred fifty plus dollars, not only had I increased my initial investment by over six hundred percent, but won the admiration of my fellow gamblers! (...with the exception of Mrs. Crankypants, of course. She was still busy tossing daggers at me with her anything-but-friendly eyes.)

Upon cashing out my winnings, I exchanged two twenty-dollar bills for more ammunition. I figured I'd simply repeat the process that brought me so much success the first time. My credits ebbed and flowed for a while, and when I glanced at my watch, I was surprised to discover it was late in the afternoon already. *Wow! Time really does fly when you're having fun!* I decided I'd play just a little longer and hopefully hit the jackpots before heading home.

I relocated to a different machine after being advised by a veteran player that the slots will often turn on a player once they've cashed out a substantial win. But luck was on my side. My winning streak continued, and each time I cashed out a hundred dollars or more, I sneaked off to the Ladies' room to tally my growing fortune in the privacy of a bathroom stall. (I didn't want to upset those less fortunate. One

Mrs. Crankypants was plenty!)

Before I knew it, evening had crept up on me. At around nine o'clock I gazed at my reflection in the bathroom mirror to find two bloodshot eyes staring back at me. It appeared as though some fairy-sized seamstress had woven tiny strands of red thread into my eyes, and then, upon closer inspection, I noticed black smudge-marks mingling with the makeup on my face.

Black filth swirled down the drain as I lathered and rinsed my hands after handling dirty coins all day. I had to repeat the process several times before they finally came clean.

Just a few more spins and I'll head home...

But a few more spins proved profitable, and it seemed only silly to leave during a winning streak. As my credits grew to well over a thousand again, I was delighted to discover that I'd become somewhat of a celebrity. A small crowd had gathered, and with each triumph, I was lavished with praise and applause. I thrived on the attention.

"Are you ever lucky!" the gentleman seated next to me said. "Rub my machine and bring me some luck, will you?" I smiled and rubbed the side of his VLT machine.

"That should do it! Any minute now..." I said, with exaggerated optimism.

The man laughed, and then whispered:

"I sure hope so. Otherwise my wife is going to kill me! Our entire mortgage payment is in this machine."

Lurking just beyond his smile was a deep sorrow, a well of anguish that likely had been building for some time. In his eyes, I saw a flicker of vulnerability, the raw truth of the matter, betraying the otherwise convincing mask that he wore.

Coincidentally, luck struck within his next few spins, and before he knew it, five red sevens were lined up on the screen before him. Landing them on a double bet, he'd earned himself an instant five hundred dollars. I was nearly knocked clean off my stool as he grabbed my shoulder and proceeded to shake the heck out of me!

Unfortunately, Mr. Lucky's excitement was to slowly dwindle away over the next couple hours, as spin by spin he bet away every credit that he'd won. He uttered not a word as he slid down from his stool to slowly walk away. I wondered how on earth he was going to tell his wife.

Close to midnight, a cocktail waitress wearing a short skirt came by with a concerned look on her face. In a kind voice she whispered, "Hey there my red-eyed friend, you really should eat something. Chicken Fingers? Fries? Seriously. You name it... it's on the house." I was surprised to realize I hadn't eaten a morsel all day, but politely declined the offer nevertheless. I was much too excited to eat. Besides, the last thing I wanted to do is muss up the slot machine's screen with greasy fingertips.

By one in the morning I felt like a disaster. My eyes burned from staring at the brightly lit screen for fourteen hours, my back and buttocks ached from hunching forward on that rock-hard barstool, and hunger pangs were beginning to take their toll.

Upon taking inventory, I noted that my credits sat just below thirty-eight hundred. I decided that I would cash out at thirty-six hundred credits or four thousand, whichever came first, and then head for home.

And then it was two o'clock, and although I'd consumed only virgin 7-Up, I felt intoxicated as I cashed out my four thousand credits. I gazed in awe at the small, paper printout. The calculation was simple, dividing by four to convert my credits into a staggering one thousand dollars. When I added this to my earlier winnings, I giggled like a schoolgirl. *Thirteen hundred smackeroos!*

I scurried over to the bartender, anxious to redeem the computer printout of my winnings. I giggled some more as he counted out my thousand dollars in twenty and fifty denominations. Never in my life had I held so much money in my hands at one time! I carefully tucked the bills into my purse alongside my earlier winnings.

In the midst of all the excitement, my instincts had somehow kicked in, so after having noticed a number of patrons witnessing the wad of money exchange hands, I decided it wise to take a few precautions. After generously tipping the bartender, I headed back into the throng of thrill-seekers still gathered about the slot machines. A tall, well-built gentleman caught my eye. I recognized him immediately, as he'd been a dedicated member of my fan club, cheering me on for more than a few hours. When I approached and asked if he'd be so kind as to escort me to my car, he told me he'd be honored.

As we approached the red Beretta waiting there beneath the blackened sky, the man offered his hand to me. "I'm Alex," he said. "Alex Williamson. I'm with Revenue Canada." A nervous laugh escaped me as I received his firm handshake. "Oh," I said. "Is that your subtle way of telling me I owe taxes on my winnings?" He chuckled. "Oh, no! Not at all! Forgive me! I guess I'm just accustomed to introducing myself while on the job." He then flattered me by saying, "I must say I admire your courage in holding out for such a big win."

I thanked the taxman for seeing me safely to my car, and, feeling wealthy and generous, slipped him a fifty for his efforts.

I arrived home to find only the front porch light on. The rest of the house was dark and silent, except for the familiar sound of Adam's snoring echoing in the hall off of our bedroom.

I simply could not contain my excitement until morning. Flicking on the bedside lamp, I took a few steps back and then sprinted forward, leaping onto the bed to startle my poor husband out of his wits. I announced my triumph by scattering my winnings all around him.

Sleep did not come easily. I tossed and turned and then tossed and turned, desperately trying to unwind from the excitement of it all. As I finally drifted off, with visions of the day's conquest replaying in my mind, I was all but oblivious to the fact that I'd just become a compulsive gambler.

13

"Forbidden Fruit"

Late the following morning my husband roused me from sleep to ask if I'd really won a hefty sum of money the day before, or if it had merely been a pleasurable dream. After confirming that yes, I had indeed won the small fortune, I remember Adam warning me not to put it all back into the machines.

Early afternoon found me in the same little pub, seated on the same rock-hard barstool, before the same VLT machine. I had elected not to heed Adam's (unsolicited) advice, as I was feeling lucky and invincible. Besides, had I not bonded with that particular machine just the day before?

Before I knew it, however, I was staring at the screen of the slot machine, wondering if the uncooperative hunk of metal had somehow developed a grudge overnight and was now out for vengeance. In two short hours, I'd lost nearly three hundred dollars!

I tried a new game... still nothing. And then frustration set in. Deciding that that stupid heap of metal was not going to get the best of me, I continued jamming money into it until *five* hundred dollars had vanished. I felt like punching the damn thing. I felt like smashing the glass, reaching in, lining up the fucking sevens, and reclaiming my five hundred dollars. My head ached, my stomach churned, and my eyeballs burned so badly I thought they might shrivel up and fall right out of my face.

Still, I was determined to win back my money.

After several failed attempts, I found myself thinking of the miserable old woman from the day before. *Why doesn't she just stop... just stop... just stop?*

I stormed out of the place, but not before gazing intently at the VLT machine with eyes narrowed, a cold whisper at my lips avowing to avenge the death of my good fortune.

I lied to my husband when he asked me how much money I'd returned to the machines. It was the first lie of my gambling career.

Before I discovered that slot machines reside not only in Vegas, but also, in the very city in which I lived, I had another form of entertainment. I enjoyed playing Bingo with a neighborhood friend. Susan could slap together a makeshift meal for three children like nobody else I knew. She would then hold dessert ransom until three "cross-my-heart" promises "not to tell daddy that mommy went out" had been extracted, all before slipping innocently out the door.

I still remember our first trip to the Bingo Hall. It was the day I received a lesson on how to drive a sports car—*my* sports car. We happened to be running late for our first Bingo session together when Susan suggested she drive my car. "Fasten your seatbelt, Darling!" she hollered, spitting gravel as she floored the gas pedal. The girl shifted gears like a seasoned racecar driver. I had no idea my little Beretta possessed such power!

Susan was a veteran of the game, able to play a fantastic

number of Bingo cards while keeping an eye on her partner's cards as well. She sat across the table from me, reaching out as needed to blot the numbers I'd missed. It was remarkable really the way she so meticulously maintained the multitude of cards, especially in light of the fact that mine lay upside down from her vantage point.

Susan and I had made a pact: any and all of our winnings would be split fifty-fifty. We'd also agreed that should either of us be so lucky as to win the "Satellite Bingo," she would be the one to jump up and yell "BINGO!" The Satellite game held the highest stakes, often in the range of fifty thousand dollars, depending on the number of participants paying into it. On numerous occasions over the months we came excruciatingly close to winning the grand prize. We captured the consolation prize a time or two, but the big jackpot remained ever elusive.

Once I discovered the vivacious VLT's scattered about the city, Bingo became but a bore. Unfortunately for me, Susan was fortunate enough to win the Satellite Bingo all by herself almost immediately after I stopped joining her.

(My friend's "good fortune" would be a bright spot in her life for only a short time however, as it would soon be overshadowed by a dark obsession to win more... and more... and more. In the weeks and months to come, a string of overdue mortgage payments would ultimately turn into the foreclosure of her home, putting her entire family out on the street, including three already neglected children.

Within a short time, Susan's husband filed for divorce, unable to accept what had happened. I imagine it would have come as quite a shock to him, seeing how his darling wife had kept it all hidden until the front door was practically hitting him in the ass on his last trip out...)

A pesky urge to play the slots arrived at a most inopportune time—right between paydays. Before I knew it my meager reserve of sixty dollars had been consumed by a VLT as if little more than an appetizer. I was determined to win back the loss, but being penniless made it difficult to proceed.

As I made my way over to Charlotte's house at the other side of town, I noticed I was precariously low on fuel. I became annoyed with myself, having squandered every cent to my name without any forethought of the consequences.

Charlotte, my dear, old atheist friend with a severe allergy to God, was away on business and had asked me to tend to her jungle of plants. First things first, I decided, as I began ransacking the house for gas money. I finally located a jar of coins on the nightstand in her son's bedroom. Relieved, I sat cross-legged on the teenager's bed and proceeded to dump the contents of the makeshift piggy bank before me. *Kid has been saving for a while*, I thought to myself, as I counted out fifty dollars in change. *Plenty enough for gas and a few spins on a VLT to recapture my earlier loss. I'll nip back and replace it before day's end...*

And with that, I raced out the door and headed for the nearest slot machine.

A miracle took place: I managed to reserve five dollars for enough fuel to get my sorry ass home.

My next visit to Charlotte's shrine of shrubbery was a mournful one. I gazed at the pitiful remains of what had once been her most treasured plant, a gift from a friend she'd lost to a car accident. It just laid there, its flowers shriveled, and its little green arms limp at its sides. Poor thing had died of thirst after the hasty departure of my last visit.

On my way home that day, after losing the money I'd "borrowed" from Charlotte's son, I'd been forced to shift my imagination into gear. Needing gas and cigarette money to get me through the next couple days, and wanting to repay the "loan" sooner rather than later, would require a plan. It wouldn't take a teenager long to miss his fifty dollars, after all.

I came up with a woeful tale of an unfortunate friend who'd had her rent money stolen in a burglary. Approaching my husband, I presented him with the sob story, asking if he'd be willing to help out my "friend." Adam agreed to help, with the condition that he be provided post-dated cheques from my friend. Of course, I gave him some excuse or another as to why she was unable to accommodate his request, not realizing that in doing so I had invoked suspicion.

With a fresh supply of money in hand I was off, determined to reclaim every cent of my lost money and then some. But before I could so much as begin plotting my strategy for the big comeback, a familiar voice was at my ear, "Just what in the hell do you think you're doing, Joan?"

I burst into tears, sobbing and shaking uncontrollably. Everyone in the place was staring. All I wanted to do was to shrivel up and die. Just like Charlotte's plant. "Alright. Calm down. Let's get out of here," Adam said, taking me by the shoulders to guide me away from the VLT machine.

I was quite surprised when my husband embraced me in the parking lot, relieved as he gently assured me that everything would be all right, that we would beat "this thing." I especially appreciated the "we" part.

Adam continued to console me even after we'd arrived home, cradling me in his arms and kissing my hair after a quick drink to calm his nerves. I could not remember a time when I'd felt so loved by my husband.

When at last my sobbing subsided, Adam proceeded with a long, drawn-out lecture on gambling. In particular, he focused on the pitfalls of slot machines, explaining how they were not, by any stretch of the imagination, designed to make the player rich. On the contrary, their sole purpose was to rob the player blind. (I was later to discover how he'd acquired such a wealth of information on the subject; after inheriting a hundred and some-odd thousand dollars from his grandfather's estate, an acquaintance of my husband's was well on his way to having inserted every last dollar into the bill slot of a VLT machine.)

I began to cry again as I told Adam how sorry I was. And then, from the bottom of my heart, a sincere promise that I would never gamble again...

...And for two, long months I kept that promise. But the day inevitably came when the urge to press that spin button had become unbearable.

This time I won't go crazy. I'll keep everything under control. Adam won't even have to know. And I believed every word I told myself. I was, after all, in a particularly lucky mood, certain I would win...

And I did win! ...but not enough ... So I spent the entire day trying to increase my winnings, right up until the very moment in which they disappeared altogether.

I don't recall how much money I lost that particular day, but I do recall the amount of self-respect and dignity I left behind.

My mind needed time to mend. I had no choice but to now consider the slot machine's oranges, cherries, and plums, "forbidden fruit." The yellow bells could toll for me no longer, and as for the seductive, red sevens... well, they would simply have to hit on someone else.

I vowed never to play the slots again, and this time, damn it, I MEANT IT!!!

Goodbye Kate

During the time I provided homecare for Kate, I was often required to go out on my own to make various purchases when she was too ill to accompany me. In order to do so, I was entrusted with my client's credit card and/or bankcard, along with the secret PIN number.

On this particular day, however, Kate Wellington was enjoying an increasingly rare reprieve from her affliction, so she took full advantage. We visited several shopping malls before enduring the mundane task of grocery shopping, then returned to the house to unpack parcels and prepare the evening meal.

John and Kate treated their home-care providers well, always mindful to make us feel at home. Tonight, after the three of us had enjoyed our delicious prime rib dinner, John turned to his wife and invited her to an evening out at the slots. Secretly, I was as thrilled as Kate was. As much as I enjoyed my job, it was trying at times, and a little solitary confinement could go a long way.

Long before I was finished enjoying my evening alone came the sound of the garage door opening. It was shortly after midnight when the Wellingtons returned from their evening out.

Kate appeared almost manic as she reached into her purse to retrieve a fist full of crumpled bills. I helped tally her winnings as she recounted for me the exciting events leading up to the great victory. I was glad my friend was able to have so much fun, and only hoped it would carry her through the unpleasantness that was sure to find her the following day.

After she'd taken her evening medication, I helped Kate prepare for bed. Once she was settled I retired to the bedroom adjacent to hers and crawled into the large, comfortable bed. The moment my head sank into the luxurious down pillow, my mind was gone; off to a casino filled with generous slot machines, where over and over and over I'd hit the jackpots.

As I drifted off to sleep I remember wishing desperately for enough money to turn the fantasy into a reality.

Kate's surgery was scheduled for late afternoon, so early morning found us scrambling to prepare for her hospital stay. With my mind entirely preoccupied with the jackpot fantasy of the night before, I found it nearly impossible to concentrate on the task at hand.

We managed to check into the hospital on time and were shown to Kate's room. I helped her get settled, organizing the few things she had brought from home. As I tucked her purse into the small, white cabinet beside the cot, I thought about returning it to the safety of her house. The considerate thought, however, lingered but a mere moment before being promptly replaced by another...

I wished my client well as she was wheeled off to surgery.

Then, after glancing up and down the hallway, I re-entered the room to dip my hand into the well-hidden purse. Withdrawing the wallet from within, I carefully extracted the blue ATM card waiting for me there in one of its tiered leather slots.

During the elevator ride to the main floor, my heart pounded so hard I was certain the other occupants could hear it.

I sat outside the hospital's main entranceway, taking in deep breaths of fresh air alternated with long draws from a cigarette. It took some time before my heart rate returned to normal, and then the tears welled. Fearing I might crack up all together, I dabbed them away before they had a chance to fall.

A stranger approached and sat next to me. I sensed her eyes on me, and a moment later, felt her hand at my back. "Did you just lose someone, Hon?" she asked, her voice warm and gentle like her hand.

"Yes, my virtue just died!" was my immediate thought.

"Oh... uh... no," I said aloud, after a few seconds had passed. "My friend just went into surgery. She's going to be just fine. But thanks all the same for asking."

Once my legs proved steady enough, I walked around the hospital lobby until I'd located an automated teller machine. I then scouted the immediate area for video surveillance cameras, breathing a sigh of relief when nothing of the sort jumped out at me. I retrieved from my pocket the blue ATM card.

Apparently my nerves hadn't quite settled yet, as my hands were anything but steady, but I did manage to key in the PIN number without incident. After glancing nervously over my shoulder, I made several experimental requests before learning how much money the card would allow. My heart thumped crazily in my chest as I collected the cash, and after reaching out a second time for the transaction printout, I was pleased to learn of the substantial amount remaining in the account.

I retrieved the pretty, blue bankcard and was gone... Off on yet another hunting expedition, determined more than ever to capture those elusive jackpots and ressurect my virtue.

The following day I made another cash withdrawal, again taking full advantage of my employer's daily cash limit. I was determined to win back the previous day's losses and replace the money I'd "borrowed," but once again, luck betrayed me.

Anxiety overwhelmed me. *How on earth am I going to fix this one?* I dreaded the thought of facing Kate when my next shift began the following day, but what absolutely terrified me... the possibility of getting caught. The mere thought of it made me cringe.

Unable to accept the prospect of such a fate, I began to analyze my predicament. Not once had I witnessed the Wellingtons fuss over finances. In fact, I could not for the life of me recall either Kate or John ever having so much as glanced at a bank statement. And surely a continuous stream of money ebbed and flowed from their abundant bank accounts, I told myself. In all likelihood the two cash withdrawals would go completely unnoticed. Before I knew it, the impending doom had faded into a mere shadow of doubt.

And then paranoia struck...

Surfing through the various news channels, my mind

replayed telecasts of culprits committing crimes to support their gambling addictions. And then there it was—my name, in BIG BOLD LETTERS—announcing to the world my identity along with every sordid detail of my transgressions. Suddenly that "mere shadow of doubt" was eclipsing every shred of my newfound confidence and then some.

Am I just being paranoid, I wondered, *or could this actually become a reality?* The daunting notion motivated me to create a foolproof plan.

Early the next day, I approached Kate as she lay in a semi-conscious state in her hospital cot. I gave her the unfortunate news that her wallet had been stolen and turned in at reception after being subsequently located in one of the hospital's public washrooms. After further explaining that I'd returned the wallet to her purse, I thoughtfully offered to take it to the safety of her house.

I felt reasonably confident that the woman's condition would prevent her from investigating my story, at least until enough time had passed for a shift-change or two to cause sufficient confusion.

My conscience, however, could not be so easily pacified. I found little solace in my victory over the bankcard ordeal, and I no longer enjoyed my job; seeing Kate was a painful reminder of my dirty deed.

Over the next few weeks I endeavored to redeem myself at the slots, but to no avail. The day inevitably arrived when guilt and shame forced me to say good-bye to Kate, and to the job I once loved so dearly.

15

Purple Pansies & More Betrayal

My next unsuspecting victim was an elderly woman of about eighty. Mrs. Carrigan suffered the usual assortment of ailments that come with old age, arthritis and the like, and found it easier to tackle day-to-day tasks with the aid of a caregiver. Money was no object, as she'd invested well the small fortune she'd acquired when her beloved husband died in the Second World War.

Dear, old Mrs. Carrigan was a pleasure to work for, rewarding even the smallest of accomplishments with generous praise. I grew quite fond of the woman, who easily filled the role of the kind grandmother I'd lost years ago.

Our routine included a weekly shopping excursion, where we would venture out to the more popular shopping malls in search of a fabulous new outfit, or whatever else happened to catch the master's eye.

The fateful day began with a brief stop at a bank where I escorted the frail Mrs. Carrigan to the wicket. I watched quietly as the friendly teller counted out her eight-hundred-dollar withdrawal. I then watched as my client carefully tucked each and every one of the crisp, new bills safely into her wallet.

Mrs. Carrigan, entirely taken with her new do, generously

tipped and thanked the hair stylist before heading off to Sears in search of the perfect outfit to complete her new look. After we'd placed our purses in the front basket of the shopping cart, Mrs. Carrigan graciously accepted the support the cart offered, holding its handle and pushing it as she strolled along.

After browsing for what seemed an eternity, Mrs. Carrigan found her heart's desire. As she held up the prized blouse for my approval, I couldn't help but think of my tired, aching feet, and, without further ado, exclaimed jubilantly that the print of vibrant purple pansies was indeed the most exquisite I had ever laid eyes on!

I placed our purses and shopping bags atop the car and gently guided my client into the passenger seat. As she fumbled with the seatbelt, I glanced at the two purses sitting just inches from my face. Without a moment's hesitation, I reached into Mrs. Carrigan's purse and withdrew her wallet. I transferred it to my own purse before sweetly offering to help fasten my client's seatbelt.

My heart pounded in my ears as I reached for the door handle. My hand was so clammy it slipped off the metal latch and I had to wipe it on my pants before a second attempt could be made.

With my mind reeling at what I'd just done, I found it a near-impossible task to drive in the rush-hour traffic while attempting to casually converse with the lady seated next to me.

Relief flooded over me as I bid Mrs. Carrigan farewell, the loss of her wallet having gone unnoticed.

By the time I pulled up in front of my house on the other side of the city, I was armed with the perfect alibi. I dialed the number of the agency that employed my services and sadly reported to Ms. Cromwell how I'd just arrived home from a shopping excursion with Mrs. Carrigan to discover my wallet missing. I suggested it might have been stolen as it sat unattended in the shopping cart during one of the brief intervals in which we turned our backs to browse. Of course, I expressed great remorse for my carelessness; invoking pity as I lamented over the inconvenience I now faced in having to deal with stolen bankcards and treasured personal effects. In closing, I expressed to Ms. Cromwell my grave concern that the same good-for-nothing bandit may also have struck dear, old Mrs. Carrigan...

Though entirely expected, the return call confirming the worst filled me with sorrow nonetheless.

The guilt was overwhelming. *Everything will be okay,* I tried to tell myself, as I headed for the nearest VLT machine. *You'll win enough to pay her back. You will replenish her wallet and turn it in at Sears' "Lost and Found" first thing in the morning...*

But before morning had a chance to arrive, my ingenius plan, along with eight hundred chances for restitution had vanished into the cold, narrow bill-slot of a VLT machine.

Working for Mrs. Carrigan became a painful ordeal. It was difficult to face her. Every time she looked at me I grew fearful that should her gaze linger, should her eyes peer into my soul but a moment longer, surely my disgraceful act would be discovered.

I explained to Ms. Cromwell that I'd decided to return to my former profession of secretarial work, asking her to convey to Mrs. Carrigan my kindest regards.

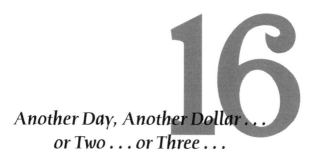

Another Day, Another Dollar . . . or Two . . . or Three . . .

Upon examining my conscience, I was horrified to discover that I'd not only become a problem gambler, but also a liar, a thief and a con artist—a most unpleasant task that "moral inventory." I vowed to avoid it at all cost from here on out. But for today the unpleasant deed was done. Perhaps today I'd had some subconscious desire to punish myself.

During my upbringing I was taught not only the basics of "right and wrong," but also, what I consider to be the utmost in moral principles. I grew up believing that lying and stealing were shameful acts committed by people with a total disregard for what is good and right. *How could such a vital part of my belief system have become so obscured? Altered beyond recognition?*

A bout of psychological warfare ensued. The intellectual side of my psyche told me that I had a problem; it was, after all, impossible to ignore the fact that I'd been doing things entirely out of character. But the affective side of my psyche (supported by my wild imagination of course) was telling me that it was all merely fallout of my recent string of bad luck, consoling me with great promise of redemption in that big win waiting just around the corner...

My guilty conscience was further appeased as I thought

of my decision to change professions. In doing so, surely I'd averted countless future "mishaps" by eliminating the temptations lurking around me.

It did not take long for me to discover that my new employer was a very understanding man. He took pity on me the day a car struck one of my dogs, going so far as to lend me the money needed for the life-saving operation. Additionally, he must have thought my car a real lemon to require so much servicing.

Often customers paid cash for merchandise and before long, temptation was once again pounding at my door. It became a constant battle to resist the readily available cash, and eventually the day came when I could resist no more.

I remember feeling utterly disgusted the day I discovered my boss dipping into the cash box. The feeling did not linger long, however. After all, who was I to judge?

Upon leaving work one afternoon, I arrived at my car to discover a note tucked beneath the windshield wiper. Lo and behold, it bore an admission from a man confessing to have scraped against my car. Upon surveying the damage I was to discover it fairly extensive, including not only an obvious scrape in the paint, but also, a broken taillight and damage to the gas tank cover. *If only I knew how to do a cartwheel...!*

I re-entered the store and called the telephone number provided in the note. Coincidentally, it turned out that Travis, the remarkably honest young man who'd left the note, was a customer of the company with which I was employed. We agreed that I would have a repair estimate done and call him back.

My husband was annoyed by the incident, but forgave my blunder just the same. I think he was just grateful that no other vehicle was involved—just his usual, reckless, pain-in-the-prat wife and one innocent steel post... Anyway, I more than made up for it, in telling him that I did not mind driving around with a little superficial damage.

Within a few days, I telephoned Travis to break the bad news. I told him that the lesser of the two repair estimates was just shy of seven hundred dollars. He took the news well, asking if I'd accept cash so he could avoid an insurance claim. *And there were cartwheels... and there was dancing...*

It was difficult to concentrate on work the rest of the afternoon. The dancing sevens and flashing red lights were such a distraction. I could almost see my exquisite red rose... smell that sweet, sweet scent of victory...

My fantasy became a reality before day's end, but it was short-lived; as usual, the dancing sevens and entourage of fruit performed to the beat of their own agenda... And it was *not* one about making *me* rich.

Paydays were painfully long. Sometimes, when I couldn't wait for the workday to end, I'd suddenly remember a doctor or dentist appointment. The second my car left the parking lot, I'd be off like a shot, racing to the nearest gambling spot to spend my hard-earned money. More often than not, the machines had appetites as insatiable as my own, gobbling up my entire paycheck within hours. I would then race home to go through the mail, setting aside any incriminating bank statements and overdue bills. In particular, I was concerned with the bank statement; it had a knack for exposing my secret gambling hideaways by showing the suspicious cash withdrawals made at their ATM machines.

What I failed to realize however, is that my resourceful husband had access to this information by simply requesting a transaction printout of our joint account at any of the five hundred conveniently located ATM machines, and was in fact, already on to me.

It came as quite a shock the day Adam confronted me with his neat little stack of evidence. As I gazed, utterly dumbfounded, at the twenty or so strips of perfectly aligned papers, it would not have surprised me in the least to discover that they were in precise order of dates, amounts of withdrawals, or bank machine numbers. *The audacity!* It absolutely infuriated me. I felt like reaching out and snatching from his hand that chatty bunch of ink-stained rat bastard papers to shuffle them to hell and back. You know, real hard, like some irate blackjack dealer... smashing them together, mashing them together... bending them, folding them, ripping them to freaking shreds... *Just who in the hell does he think he is?!*

If I freaked *right* out, and yelled louder than my husband, he would usually back down from the fight. Oh, no-no... Not in a wimpy way! There was absolutely nothing wimpy about my husband. I'd say it was more about a rare, admirable quality he possessed where he could recognize his own limitations. Somehow he knew when he'd reached his boiling point, knew when to walk away before things got really nasty. I'm sure I caught onto this early, and did not hesitate to take advantage—unless I was too weak to fight. Sometimes, after days without any real food, only 7-Up and potato chips, and next to no sleep, I would just shut up and take it, cower in the corner and allow my husband to verbally kick the crap out of me. But if I'd recently had a decent meal, perhaps in celebration of a win at the slots, followed by a well-deserved sleep, the kind without machete-wielding bill collectors threatening to lop off my spin-button finger or greedy slot machines with suction-cup tentacles so callous and sneaky that they would simply slither on up and glop onto my golden dollars before I could *think* to drop them into the slot... It was then that a resolve great enough to conquer the enemy was easy to come by. Or sometimes, when Adam would pick a fight during a most annoying losing streak, when I was hungry, tired, and perhaps a tad more insane than usual... a pent-up rage like no other was bound to come undone.

I could get very ugly when confronted about my gambling. It was almost like in the horror movies, where the demon-possessed are being exorcised, and their mouths fly open to spew out all kinds of vile obscenities, and threats, and accusations, often in a voice not of their own making. Poor Adam... In a span of about sixty seconds I'd have taken the guy's entire inventory, including many unkind remarks about his sexual performance, or lack thereof. Entirely undeserved of course... at least for the most part... but man, did it do the trick! *How'd ya like that Jerk-face? Teach you to mess with the VLT Queen!*

Sometimes I'd apologize... usually right after my next win.

Guess Adam didn't get too many apologies...

A PLACE WHERE WEEDS & ROSES GROW

17

Substitute Children

Despite my many behaviors to the contrary, I still claim to have possessed some basic common sense. For example, I understood the concept of paying bills. My struggle was with the notion of taking care of those boring old living expenditures before first trying to double or triple my money. Although the concept failed me miserably more often than not, landing me little more than a generous stack of overdue bills, I could not let it go. For some reason, the insanity of it all did not register. I'd merely blame my predicament on bad luck, believing that at any moment it would turn around. After all, I'd been lucky in the past. And all I really needed was that one BIG WIN. Surely it could not evade me indefinitely...

I remember vividly the day Adam arrived home from work earlier than expected. He'd been injured, and upon his employer's insistence, was forced to miss out on that day's OT. Normally, he'd have duct-taped the gaping wound back together and carried on as though nothing had happened, but apparently this time it just wasn't meant to be so; a co-worker had witnessed the accident and promptly tattled to the boss.

Also itching to tattle was an overdue bill from that

day's mail. (My husband took care of our largest payments—mortgage, personal loan and credit cards, while I took care of the smaller items—utilities, insurance and groceries.) It sat atop the dining room table like a lit stick of dynamite, its fuse growing shorter and shorter by the second...

My heart skipped a beat as I heard my husband's footsteps approach the back door. Quick as a flash, I snatched up the incriminating evidence to stuff it beneath the ghetto blaster on the floor. I then watched as Adam fixed himself a "Rye and Coke," breathing a sigh of relief only when he was well past the hidden bill and half stretched over the living room sofa.

As fate would have it, however, my husband awoke in an extra ambitious mood but a day later and began vacuuming the house. He was always *extremely* thorough when he cleaned, finding every speck of dirt in every nook and cranny. Not one dust-mite could escape the madman with the sucking machine.

Watching in horror as the spinning brushes of the power-head loomed ever closer to the little black music box, I cursed myself for being so careless. Then, as my husband stooped over to move it, I fled the room, unable to face the music.

Perhaps he never confronted me about the overdue bill because finding them hidden around the house was his only hope of learning when the power or phone was to be disconnected.

What started out as mere entertainment had somehow manifested into a full-blown addiction. I no longer had time for my friends or to enjoy the simple things in life. I was too busy treading water in my ever-expanding sea of lies and deceit, weighted down by debt and denial.

How long before I'm completely submerged? Will I pull my husband down with me?

Before gambling became an all-consuming obsession, occupying every spare minute I had, I used to take great pleasure in spending time with my dogs. Missy and Oreo were our substitute children. Entirely delightful they were, although somewhat relentless in their quest for love and attention. I called them my "Super-absorbent Love Sponges."

Having been adopted first, Missy instinctively assumed the role of "Pack Leader" when young Oreo came along. It proved no small challenge, however, to force the newcomer into submission; turned out the adorable coat of black and white fur was merely camouflage to a most rebellious pup. But Missy persevered, and after a constant, gentle scolding and outpouring of motherly love, the tiny terror finally relented. Missy assumed her rank as Captain, rightfully displaying her tail at high-mast, while Oreo took up position of Commander, tail sitting at half-mast.

They grew inseparable over the years, living out the typical dog's life side by side as they ate together, slept together and played together. Both being Border Collies, they could almost pass as identical twins, their physical differences so subtle most people could not tell them apart. Each of the girls' personalities, however, had traits uniquely her own.

Missy was about as prim and proper as a pooch can get, displaying the utmost in canine etiquette. Gingerly, she nibbled one piece of gourmet dog food at a time, drinking water in an equally dainty fashion, rarely allowing so much as a drop to dribble down her chin. She was every inch a lady, from the tip of her pointy nose to the tip of her fancy tail. So ladylike was she that she graciously removed herself from public viewing to pass gas in a private place. (I'd concluded this after years of never once having witnessed the great event.)

Oreo, on the other hand, was a tomboy through and through. Surely, not the slightest trace of femininity ran in those tomboy veins of hers. Like a shark at a feeding frenzy she'd attack her food, only to lurk in the shadows afterwards, anxious to devour any morsel remaining in Missy's dish. She gulped from the water bowl as though it were her last, drooling a steady stream down her chin before leaving a trail of puddles as she sauntered away. Oh, and yes... Oreo was far from bashful about passing gas in front of an audience.

Poor Missy suffered the occasional bout of neurosis. Fear gripped her as she sensed the imminent danger lurking within the black storm clouds; her body would begin to vibrate and her legs would grow stiff as she anxiously paced the floor, her long, pink tongue rolling out over her teeth to initiate a bout of nervous panting.

The first clap of thunder startled her, and with eyes widening in terror, she'd spring from the floor to land in the safety of my lap. Like a cat clinging to a tree for dear life, Missy would curl her claws into my legs and bury her face between my knees. Every fiber of her being trembled within that fur coat, and although I made every effort to reassure her, only when that angry rumbling in the sky decided to quiet itself, would my frightened pet return to normal.

Not a single ice-cream truck could penetrate our security system without detection. With a hair-raising howl from the back porch Missy would sound the alarm, warning the entire neighborhood of the menace in the street. She was appeased only when either my husband or I would approach the ice-cream man, reprimand him for trespassing on her territory, and then return to her with a much-deserved ice-cream treat.

We did not have a fly swatter adorning a wall in our home. Ohhh no! Only a fortunate few flies ever escaped the sudden death grip of the "Missy Flytrap." With each victory, she pranced about, her head held high, and her tongue thrashing wildly as she desperately attempted to rid herself of the fly's remains.

Some people say that dogs inherit their masters' personality traits. Miss Oreo had an obsessive-compulsive disorder. Her life's ambition was to "clean the clock" of every dog that lived and breathed within a hundred-mile radius. The entire earth was her domain and hers alone. She tolerated sharing it with her "sister" only out of respect for the natural laws of the canine world where Missy happened to get first dibs.

Another of Oreo's obsessions was the tennis ball. The green felt-covered object lay patiently in wait for its master during mealtime, later to accompany her to bed, where it would thoughtfully position itself within reach, should Oreo stir in the dead of night with an urge to play.

Oreo loved her ball with a passion. After every game of fetch, after chasing down and chomping on the ball over and over and over, she'd gently position it between her front paws to lovingly kiss it a hundred times. Only when the ball forgave her for inflicting such cruel and unusual punishment would the game resume.

Sometimes, in the middle of all of my gambling insanity, I'd just stop and stare... And sometimes, for a brief, merciful moment in time, everything would just fall away... everything except for those funny, funny dogs and their funny ways. And sometimes I'd smile, and it felt so good... And then I'd see them looking at me; wondering, perhaps, why *I* was acting so funny. *Who are you?* their eyes would ask... *Who are you, and why aren't you out gambling?*

The more preoccupied I became with gambling, the more Missy and Oreo began to act up. I'd return home from a gambling excursion to find plastic bags pulled out from the cupboard and shredded over the kitchen floor, or the bathroom garbage strewn from one end of the hall to the other. It was their way of letting me know that I was neglecting them. I felt bad for hurting my beloved canine pals, so I decided to start taking them for walks again.

Missy and Oreo could barely contain their excitement as I tied the laces of my tennis shoes. They danced around like circus animals, wagging their tails and barking, pleading with me to hurry up and get the show on the road.

They scrambled into the backseat of the car where they bounced from side to side, anxious to get to their favorite off-leash park where a long overdue adventure awaited them. It had been a while, so they were quite frantic about the whole thing, yipping out the windows as though I were pinching them the entire way.

Dogs of every shape and size frequented the large, off-leash park. It was ideally situated, with a river running parallel to the walking path. The path itself stretched for several miles and was partnered with huge open fields filled with all sorts of exciting dog-smells and critters to chase around.

Missy and Oreo continued chomping at the bit, eager to join the myriad other dogs and chase their ball until they could run no more. Then, finally, with every last ounce of energy spent, they'd head for the crisp, cool waters below. There, they would sprawl out over the smooth rock-bed in the shallows, cooling their spent bodies and quenching their thirst at long last.

But before we could get there, the car took an unexpected detour. Within minutes, we were parked below a large sign hollering down at us:

WE'VE GOT THE SEVEN LUCKIEST VLT'S!

Wouldn't be long before I'd come to realize just how literally I should have taken those six enticing words...

The sun was beating down from a cloudless sky, a sure sign of a sweltering hot day. I became even more aware of the growing heat the moment I turned the ignition to the off position. *Don't worry—it won't take but a minute to hit the bells or sevens,* the urge whispered seductively. I hopped out of the car so fast I nearly strangled myself with the still-fastened seatbelt.

The alarmed voice of a barmaid sounded. At first I wanted to knock her block off, hollering like that. Or at least stitch up her lips. There was nothing more annoying than a blabbermouth breaking a player's concentration; especially when that player was getting her ass kicked all over the place.

Shut up! Shut up! SHUT UUUUP!

And then her words began to register.

Red car...

Two dogs...

As I whipped my head around to claim ownership, the look of concern on the young woman's face turned to an angry scowl and as she came at me, I half-expected to have *my* block knocked off. In no uncertain terms, she proceeded to accuse me of being a stupid fucking bitch and a dog-abuser.

Everyone in the place glared at me as I raced out the door.

I arrived at the car to find my dogs trying to claw their way out through the windows. Glancing at my watch, I was overcome with guilt, as I realized I'd left them trapped in the car for over two hours without water or attention. At least I'd thought to leave the air-conditioning on. *Thank God I hadn't run out of gas...*

Without hesitation, I reached for the door handle and pulled the door open. Missy and Oreo leapt out from the backseat and onto the hot asphalt, and as I coaxed them towards a small, grassy area shaded by large trees, I realized my entire body was trembling.

I knelt before my dogs, kissing and stroking their heads, sobbing and begging for their forgiveness.

After making amends as best I could, my girls still refused to return to the car. Eventually, I had to pick them up, one at a time, and physically place them into the vehicle.

I was so worn out after fighting a losing battle with the "lucky" slot machine and causing my dogs such grief that I simply headed for home. There would be no fun at the dog-park today, and it would be a long time before Missy and Oreo would willingly get into my car.

18

From the Bowels of Hell

By now my husband was more than a little fed up with my gambling. He was tired of driving around looking for me at all hours of the day and night. He was tired of overdue bills and pitiful excuses. He was tired of my sleeping in during the workweek, and tired of eating out of cans (alternated with boxes of KD) after a hard day's work. To sum it up, my husband was sick and tired of living in the hell that was our marriage. I would imagine his definition of hell to be, 'A place where your wife is obsessed with gambling and will lie to you, steal from you, and stab you in the back to get her fix.'

Adam grew up on a large farm where backbreaking work was a given and anything over and above the bare necessities, a luxury. Being ranked second in command amid five siblings and with meager means to support such a large family, Adam had learned to appreciate the true value of a dollar. He despised debt and strongly believed that the only respectable way to acquire material wealth was to work hard and come by it honestly. Squandering money to support a gambling habit was simply inconceivable.

Adam was a realist. He was scientifically minded and expected things to make "sense." He was honest to a fault (if there really is such a thing) and believed in all that is good and right and just. Wow, was he in for the surprise of his life the day he asked me to dance! ...

I had started up a small company with a friend of mine selling sportswear and the like and was in possession of the checkbook and bankcard. This came in handy when, once again, the inevitable day arrived when I'd not a penny to my name, only a persistent desire to hit the jackpots on a slot machine.

So I deposited a cheque written against our business account into the same account and withdrew the cash. I felt confident that within hours I would win not only enough to cover the NSF cheque, but enough to have a tidy profit left over.

By day's end I was in an utter state of shock; I'd lost every cent along with every hope of reversing the illegal bank transaction. I had no choice but to tell my husband.

As I begged Adam to bail me out, he flew into a rage like nothing I'd ever seen. Every vein in the man's head popped out and as he hollered and pounded the table, I couldn't help but wonder if I might be next. But by some miracle, Adam was always able to restrain himself.

After giving in to "the absolute final bailout," Adam's anger turned to grief. It broke my heart to see that tough, rugged man who was my husband break down and cry. It almost made me want to stop gambling.

Almost.

Sick and tired of not having a steady supply of money to play with, I could not believe my good fortune when a credit card application arrived in the mail. Although it was addressed to the only person in our household with sufficient income, the industrious, young fellow known also as my husband, of course, my excitement soared nonetheless.

Without hesitation, I filled in all the required information, taking the liberty to name myself secondary cardholder of course, before finishing it off with a mighty fine forgery (if I don't say so myself) of hubby's signature. I practically skipped to the mailbox.

For three grueling weeks I waited for that card. It felt like forever. I pretty much camped out next to the mailbox, guarding it with my life.

And then there it was...

Determined to keep things under control, my first cash advance was a modest three hundred dollars. I must say, I was quite pleased with my ingenuity, but then, as I began spending the "well-deserved" money, a twinge of guilt arose from my heart of hearts. I'd really crossed a line this time. I was about to strike it rich and have my happily ever after (surely my husband would forgive me if I won a ton of money), *or else...*

I remember the woman seated a few machines down from me. She really stood out as she fed the bill slot of her gambling machine one twenty after another, all the while appearing entirely perplexed and loudly exclaiming, "I just can't seem to stop! What the dickens is wrong with me? I just can't seem to stop!"

Glancing at the poster on the wall above the slot machines, I read to myself the bold printed message I'd read a hundred times before. IF YOU HAVE A GAMBLING PROBLEM, CALL 1-800-665-9676. My immediate thought: *Gee, she should really call and get some help, for goodness sakes!*

My initial three-hundred-dollar investment vanished into

a greedy slot machine. After scraping the final few unlucky coins from the bottom of my purse, I began to hunt down the ATM.

On my next trip to the automated teller machine a short time later, I was annoyed to be informed that I'd reached my credit card's daily cash limit and would be getting not a penny more. I couldn't decide whether to cry or rip my fucking hair out. Likely, I did a little of both...

I must have appeared a raving lunatic to anyone who may have witnessed any one of my temper tantrums. Often, I would manage to refrain from exploding until I'd reached my car... then all hell broke loose... *literally.* I'd pummel the steering wheel with my fists and spew out obscenities so foul they could only have been harvested straight from the bowels of hell. Sometimes I'd glare into the rearview mirror to call myself the "C" word. And sometimes I'd threaten to kill that stupid you-know-what glaring back at me.

Sometimes after a loss I would make my way to my car to ball my hand into a fist and pretend to punch myself in the head. Depending on how big the loss was, sometimes my rock-hard fist would connect. It hurt, but it felt so good that often I would do it again... and again. *How do you like that you stupid loser-bitch?!* And then I'd cry all the way home, desperate for that moment of relief when my aching head would fill with yet another foolproof plan for redemption... And when that foolproof plan refused to materialize and my rage returned with a vengeance, my hand would again clench up, this time to pound against my chest over and over, as I plunged the imaginary knife deeper and deeper into my stupid body. Sometimes I'd laugh afterwards. I'm not sure why.

To avoid detection, I learned to park my car in cluttered

side streets and unlit back alleys, sometimes being forced to walk in the rain or cold and often in the black of night. (The idea of getting sick or being assaulted, or worse, bothered me not in the least. In fact, at times, I may have even *welcomed* such "punishment.")

I recall parking in the lot of a busy grocery store located across the street from the bar I was visiting one day. Oh so cleverly, I parked smack dab in the middle, camouflaging my car amid the myriad others. *Tee hee hee! I could go undetected for hours!*

Unfortunately, for some mind-boggling reason, the grocery store did not stay open until 2 a.m. Although my eyes were not functioning well after staring at the VLT screen for so long, twenty-twenty vision would not be required to locate my car. Nope. A one-eyed guy with a blindfold would have had little difficulty! There it was, sticking out like a gigantic sore thumb, all alone in the otherwise deserted parking lot.

I cannot see well without the aid of corrective lenses and, unfortunately, am not a good candidate for contacts. Feeling less than attractive when sporting a pair of framed eyeglasses, I often chose vanity over practicality, refusing to wear my glasses in public. It was nerve-racking en route to my gambling destinations, as one white work-van after another would appear—each resembling that of my husband! It bugged me to no end that Adam's boss was too stingy to have the company name put on his van.

Paranoia began to get the best of me, so I began taking alternate routes, often winding up lost in the endless maze of side streets and cul-de-sacs that make up half the city. What a colossal waste of gambling time!

My less than perfect vision caused me a lot of grief while

playing the slots as well. Oh, I could see the machine's screen perfectly well... no worries there... but trying to visually 'screen' the endless flow of patrons coming through the door was another matter entirely. Every other person appeared to be my husband! Like a deer in the headlights I gawked at every man resembling Adam, my heart racing frantically in my chest. More often than not men would interpret my wide-eyed gaze as an open invitation, approaching with their vast array of come-ons. I would simply confess the truth; that I'd forgotten my eyeglasses and had mistaken them for my husband. This usually caused them to flee in a hurry.

Apparently I was too busy having an affair with a slot machine to have one with a human being...

As far back as I can remember I've had less than sufficient bladder control. I do manage quite well without absorbent undergarments... let's make that perfectly clear! I simply have to respond within a short time of nature's call to avoid a potential accident. This, however, was no small challenge when seated before a hot slot machine. *Just one more spin, just one more chance; just one more 'til I pee my pants...* Often, I would delay a visit to the Ladies' Room until I was struggling to maintain control, until I was awkwardly writhing in my seat. I'm surprised no one ever suggested I try some Preparation H.

Christmas has always been my favorite time of the year. Of course, as a youngster, it was all about pretty lights and presents, but as my spiritual awareness matured it became less about me and more about the blessed birth of my Lord and Savior. It became a time for reflection and celebration, a time for love and laughter, family, and friends. At no other time of the year did my heart feel so contented. All the trials and tribulations of the past eleven months seemed to disappear, as though God himself had snatched them away.

And then the gambling started.

Christmas became the time of year I dreaded most. I'd somehow gotten it in my head that it was necessary to lavish everyone with an expensive gift. Somewhere along the way, my Jesus had fallen to the wayside. The days leading up to the once joyous occasion were now spent sweating in front of a slot machine trying to hit the jackpots and, eventually, trying to win back enough money to hit the dollar store on the way home. Gambling had become for me (quite literally), *The Grinch Who Stole Christmas.*

Not unlike my faith, my dignity and dreams along with everything else that made me who I was, were fast disappearing into the fathomless hellhole that was my life as a compulsive gambler.

So far I'd managed to keep my gambling problem a secret from my parents. In fact, I'd convinced them that my "occasional" gambling excursion was nothing more than a little "harmless, recreational fun."

They came to visit one weekend when I happened to have a small accumulation of recent wins. Mom and dad arrived (unannounced) on a Friday, which was doubly annoying, as I had planned that evening to use my small purse of winnings to hit the jackpot. I managed somehow to get through the evening without a meltdown, but by the following morning, there was no curbing my appetite...

My dear, sweet mother looked so out of place in that dingy little bar. A haze of cigarette smoke hovered overhead, and down below, a threadbare carpet struggling to conceal evidence of barroom brawls long seeped into the porous gray cement. From the beginning, I'd frequented only the seediest places I could find, certain to remain anonymous. Sure I was often mistaken for the stripper next door by the slobbering drunk of the hour who'd been lusting after me since the moment I'd tossed my garter his way, but better him "recognizing" me than my husband or boss...

It was not easy, but with my mother looking on, I forced myself to refrain from sliding a handful of twenties into the bill-slot. Instead, I very sparingly dropped a handful of Loonies (Canadian one-dollar coins) into the coin-slot to make only modest twenty-five cent bets. But before anything exciting could transpire, the cigarette smoke got to my mother and we were on our way out the door. Oh, well. Not much hope of striking it rich on twenty-five cent bets anyway.

I remember vividly the drive home, my mother's gentle warning not to get "carried away" with gambling. Of course, I merely dismissed her concern; was she not, after all, just being her typical mother-hen-self, fretting over everything?

19

The Man with the Halo

Never in a million years could I have imagined that I would one day commit Insta-bank fraud and forge someone's signature to obtain a credit card. Never in a billion years could I have imagined that I wouldn't stop there...

I sat on the living room sofa staring out the window as though at any moment the solution to all my problems might magically appear. And then there it was! Often, I twirled my wedding rings while deep in thought. Maybe that had a little something to do with it...

When the notion first arrived, with it came several conflicting emotions—at the onset I felt elated, excited at the prospect of having such a large amount of cash at my disposal; but then, before I could soar too, too high, apprehension and fear yanked me back down to earth. It was like having a nasty vat of stomach acid dumped over my happy butterflies. Not that that mattered, really. Enough of them would survive to band together and overcome any fear or apprehension still lingering about...

I made cue cards and rehearsed my story until it was about as flawless as my diamond, then reached for the cordless phone. I remember my finger trembling as I keyed in the telephone number. And I remember the high, that delicious surge of adrenaline coursing through my veins, growing stronger and stronger with each additional ring. It was not unlike the high I got while watching my colorful shapes spinning, spinning on a VLT screen.

The insurance guy was very accommodating, sympathetic to a fault, really. Not exactly what I'd expected. In fact, I was left feeling both repulsed by the man's stupidity, and scared spitless that he was merely a better actor than I was.

I hung up the phone and paced a hole in the floor. I nearly lost my nerve, considered calling the guy back to tell him it was all a mistake, that I'd remembered where I'd put my ring. And then I thought of the money... *Five thousand dollars!* (less the deductible). Plenty enough to win back all my previous losses and then some! I could pay everyone back and get caught up on bills. Heck, I could even buy a gift for everyone, a nice gift, and pay next month's bills in advance! Imagine that! I'd probably win a prize! I decided it best that my ring remain lost...

The insurance fellow had offered me two choices: I could go down and pick my cheque up, or have him toss it into the mail. I'd opted for picking it up; told him I'd be in first thing the following day. The moment I hung up the telephone, however, I found myself glancing at the clock. *What the hell were you thinking, girl?* I practically shouted at myself.

Grabbing hold of the receiver, I pressed redial and asked to speak with Mr. Goodman again. I took a deep breath and, trying not to sound overly anxious, asked if it were possible to have a cheque cut immediately. He told me that yes, he would be happy to accommodate my request, adding jovially, "Careful you don't get a speeding ticket now. We carry your car insurance, too, you know!"

I felt dizzy with excitement.

And then paranoia struck.

Is he on to me? Is that why he was so insanely cheerful? Was he just giddy about catching a crook? Are the cops going to be waiting there for me? Could I go to jail for this?

I told myself to stop being ridiculous, how could he possibly know? ... but the uneasiness stayed with me.

Not until I was back behind the wheel with the cheque in hand did I start to believe I might actually get away with it; even then, I wondered if my heart would ever stop pounding. Eventually it returned to a more normal rhythm, and I even managed a giggle or two after successfully maneuvering my way out from the downtown core without a cop in my rearview mirror.

I deposited the cheque into the ATM and withdrew my maximum daily cash allowance. My heart began to race again, but this time I didn't mind so much.

I couldn't get to the bar fast enough (get the hell out of my way pedestrians!). And then... *sweet relief.* It felt so-o-o-o good to escape, to crawl into the screen of that VLT machine and just forget... if only for a while...

My heart continued its marathon for several hours, before being utterly pulverized by defeat. But, oh well. I'd recover. There was always tomorrow. Tomorrow I could withdraw another grand. Or maybe I'd march my ass right into the bank and withdraw the remaining three and a half thousand. Better safe than sorry.

I was so tired of being sorry.

I'm not entirely sure how much time passed before I got the phone call. I'd venture a guess of two weeks... perhaps three.

Some of the lesser important details are a bit fuzzy. Anyway, it wasn't long after I'd lost every penny of the almost five thousand dollars I'd scammed from the insurance company that the call came. My first thought was *Wow! He really does love us unconditionally!* God, that is. I actually thought he was behind it, a helping hand to pull me out from my latest pit of despair.

"Ma'am, I'm calling to inform you of some good news. Good news for *you,* that is. It appears we've made a bit of a blunder. Apparently we shorted you just shy of five hundred dollars on your recent insurance claim." I'm sure I heard the gentle strum of harps in the background.

I did not respond. I think I went into shock or something. How many times had I heard of their underhanded maneuvering; insurance companies exposed again and again for the no good so-and-so's that they are... shamelessly denying the claims of their most faithful clients simply because they can?

"Ma'am? Ma'am? Are you still with me? Hello?"

...And now this! However did I miss the halo? Thing must have been the size of Saturn's ring for goodness sakes!

I finally responded and the man was able to proceed with some long drawn-out explanation as to the discrepancy in my recent pay out. As the heavenly voice began to drone on, I became restless... *Just give me my money already!* (Really and truly—did the details matter? I was just glad it was not the other way around, with me owing *them* the five hundred dollars. *Get in line Bud... Get in line.*)

He shamed me with his honesty. I remember for a brief time after I'd hung up the telephone just sitting there with my hands folded in my lap, staring out the window in disbelief.

As much as I wanted to believe the money a gift from God, a chance to redeem myself, I knew deep down it was nothing of the sort.

The guilt hit hard and fast and made me sob uncontrollably. But it wouldn't last long—before I could so much as reach for a Kleenex my guilt had turned to elation. And long before shame and remorse could weasel their way into my conscience, I was gone, out the door like some lunatic with a gambling problem to collect yet another batch of tainted money.

Sometime later, I was watching *Sixty Minutes* or *The Fifth Estate*, or one of those informative-type programs, where they were showing videotaped footage of supposed back-injured insurance recipients. One was doing back-flips off a diving board, another, lugging new furniture into his home. I scoffed at them.

And then it dawned on me... *I'm no different than they are!* And with that came an onslaught of guilt, shame and remorse, seeping deep, deep into my conscience like a fast-moving cancer. I did not fight it this time. It was cruel and relentless and ate at me until I thought I'd crawl right out of myself.

I wished I could just disappear.

Into a VLT machine.

Forever.

A PLACE WHERE WEEDS & ROSES GROW

20

Not-So-Fun Dominoes

Before things had gotten entirely out of control, to the point where my addiction had taken over my entire being (except a brain cell or two, perhaps, and maybe, just maybe a lonesome moral tucked away snug in some deep, dark cranny), I remember waking up on a few weekend mornings desperate *not* to gamble. It was the strangest thing, really. From out of nowhere came these overwhelming panic attacks, manic panic almost—a sensation so strong that it forced me to hop out of bed and race to the back door to barricade my husband's escape route.

I would beg Adam to spend the day with me, tossing out all kinds of inviting activities; *hiking at Kananaskis with the dogs, a barbecue with friends—I'll even buy the beer! No? Well... okay... how about some S E X* (wink-wink, complete with crazy hair & morning breath). *Or how about a long drive to the middle of nowhere... freaking nowhere... anywhere... somewhere we've never been... somewhere we've been a thousand times... Ohhh, come on! Haven't you always wanted to see Antarctica?*

I DON'T CARE WHERE, DAMN IT... JUST AS LONG AS THERE ARE NO VLT's THERE!

Perhaps the peculiar urges not to play the machines hadn't come out of 'nowhere,' but rather, arrived on the heels of a nightmare. I can't recall for sure. But it would certainly explain things. At about the same speed as my addiction, my nightmares too were growing progressively worse. Often I would awaken from one with such intense anxiety that it would take half the morning for me to calm down. Especially if I'd had bad luck the night before. If it happened that I'd won the night before, I'd simply get up and count my winnings a time or two or three and... voila! No more anxiety! Just like magic. Too bad those happy, abracadabra moments were so gosh-darned few and far between.

Perhaps those rare moments of (anxious) clarity where I'd had no desire to gamble were a manifestation of an innate instinct for survival, a (subconscious) last-ditch effort to save myself? All that was certain was the feeling of desperation, of not wanting to spend another second in front of a slot machine.

Lord, Lord, may those feelings be forever etched into my psyche... fresh, raw and real; an ever-present portrait to remind me of the horrors...

More often than not, my husband would continue on out the door as though I was invisible. I do, however, recall one occasion when he relented...

The weather could not have been more perfect—not too hot, not too cold—not that the dogs would have complained one iota had there been an all out blizzard in the works. So away we went to the off-leash park, the girls and I in the Beretta, my husband in his big, burly van... (Adam insisted he be able to leave directly from the park to go to work. No point in wasting a good ten minutes of valuable work time for goodness sake.)

My idea of going to Southland Park, and I'm quite sure

Missy and Oreo would have concurred, was to spend a few quality hours wandering aimlessly through the vast, open meadows, tossing the ball every now and then, chasing the odd gopher or two (or three), all before leisurely making our way down to the Sip-n-Dip River Inn Café for some self-serve refreshments.

Adam liked speed walking... that and asking for the time every five minutes. I wished I'd forgotten my wristwatch at home. It was unlikely he'd ask someone else. My husband wasn't one for talking to strangers—or to me, for that matter. Unless he wanted to know what time it was.

Regardless, I remember feeling almost giddy. *Fresh air... two happy dogs... no slot machines in sight... long-lost husband at my side...*

I couldn't help myself... Reaching out, I clamped onto Adam's hand to hold it lovingly with my own. Immediately, his face began to scrunch up, and before I knew it, he'd stopped dead in his tracks. Had there been a few more people on the narrow pathway, we likely would have gone down like dominoes. *My* face likely scrunched up a tad too as Adam proceeded to shake his hand loose from mine. And then, before I could say *please don't make a scene!* he was shaking it about the air... *vigorously* shaking it about the air! It looked as though he was trying to rid himself of some sort of flesh eating bacteria. Hardly embarrassing at all.

Needless to say, my sudden desire for a hiatus from the gambling was short lived. Turned out I needed a hiatus from the hiatus... me, my tarantula and my Ebola Virus.

It came as no great surprise the day my husband moved into

the basement. And, to be perfectly honest, I didn't mind at all. I'd always hated having to tiptoe into the bedroom in the wee hours of morning. Especially when I'd do such a magnificent job, taking all the time in the world tip-tip-tip-toeing across the carpet, far outdoing the quietest church mouse that ever lived, to peel back my corner of the blankets *ohhh so gently,* as though I were the sure bet in a slow-motion, giant Band-Aid removal contest, only to be greeted by, "Where the fuck *were you?!*" I'd nearly jump clean out of my freaking skin.

21

Toothless Tom

After struggling for two long years to stay afloat, the small company I was working for finally went under. Fortunately, I was able to secure a promising position at the head office of a fast food franchising company almost immediately afterwards.

At my new place of employment I made it a point not to tell a soul about my gambling. I wasn't about to jeopardize a potential chance to borrow money. In particular, I kept it hidden from the fellow inhabiting cubicle three; intuition told me he had an extra soft spot for damsels in distress.

Just as I'd suspected, Marshmallow Boy was the first in line to offer assistance the dreadful day my hot water tank died. Everyone expressed sympathy as I described the ice-cold shower I'd been forced to suffer through that morning, but it was little old Leroy who'd so kindly offered to lend me the eight hundred dollars necessary to purchase a new tank. (Thankfully he did not realize—any more than I did at the time—that a decent hot water tank can be purchased for less than half that amount.)

I'd planned to use the newly acquired cash to win back my previous losses and get my finances in order, but, surprise-surprise, it didn't quite work out that way. In the end, I managed only to dig myself deeper into debt.

I found it such an annoyance having to pay him back. Not only was I faced with a bothersome credit card payment each month, but now, also, the additional hassle of yet another debt. Had I not racked up my credit card with all of those useless cash advances, I could have simply charged the new hot water tank. Entirely irrelevant of course, seeing how there was absolutely nothing wrong with the tank we already had.

Not only had I become a compulsive gambler, but a compulsive liar as well. It made me feel dirty and loathsome. A part of me died every time I deceived someone. Especially my family and close friends. I didn't deserve them... or my husband. *And they certainly did not deserve me.*

When Adam began asking where all the money was going, I decided it time to tell him about the loan shark. He was your typical shady character, you know, six foot something, dark hair, in desperate need of some dental work. Met him at a bar a few months back, I'd explained, during a particularly bad spell at the slots. He was seated next to me, and eventually struck up a conversation. The guy seemed sincere enough, so I shared with him my sad tale of woe, going so far as to tell him how I was in way over my head and if my luck didn't turn around soon I'd be in more trouble than I could handle. The guy offered to help, suggesting that he provide me a loan at a reasonable rate, enough to pay off all my gambling debts. No strings attached. He seemed sincere enough, I told my husband, and really, what options did I have left?

I sobbed as I told Adam how the mean man turned on me, forcing me to repay him twice the original loan. I went on to assure him that it was over now, that the money had been repaid in full and I had warned the guy that if he harassed me further I would not hesitate to call the police. At this point, I'd rather hoped that my husband would have been so relieved that no harm had come to his precious wife that he'd simply have forgiven me, maybe even thrown his arms around me a while. But Adam was no dummy; he knew full well that his wife had never been in any real danger. After all, Toothless Tom was merely a figment of her imagination; conjured up to explain the lack of money and hang-up calls. Hang-up calls which, oddly enough, occurred only when Adam answered the telephone...

Sometime prior, I'd struck up a friendship with a fellow gambler; a decent enough guy who'd shared my passion for playing slot machines. Larry was an oilman from Texas, flying into Calgary on business once or twice a month. It was apparent the oil industry was good to him; an expensive-looking wristwatch and pair of exotic reptilian boots confirmed it. And Larry was anything but stingy with his good fortune, insisting on treating me to lunch and dinner along with an endless supply of 7-Up, the hardest drink I ever ordered. (I think the whole Manic-Tequila thing had done me in.)

Often, when my money ran out and I bid my friend farewell, he would slip a twenty into the VLT's bill-slot and say, in his fancy, albeit somewhat exaggerated, accent, "Come now girl, y'all don't wanna be desertin' me whilst ya still got credits on yer machine, now do ya?" The first few times I politely declined his offer, insisting that I had to 'git my butt on home,' but eventually the man's generous offers became irresistible.

Sometimes when I hit the sevens Larry would casually

reach out and rub my back as he congratulated me. As time passed, the backrubs grew less and less casual and, somewhere along the way, turned into lengthy embraces. Sometimes his eyes would meet mine and linger there just long enough to make me turn away in shyness. *Or was that guilt?*

One evening, after enjoying a profitable day at the slots, Larry treated me to dinner at one of the city's finest restaurants. It was an elegant place; lights way down low, the flicker of candlelight casting a soft glow, and a slow, soothing melody providing the final, intimate touch.

We gazed at one another in the soft, golden light. Larry told me I looked like an angel. Funny... *I didn't feel like an angel...*

As we waited for our meals to arrive, we enjoyed a few quiet laughs, and then grew serious as we spoke of the loneliness in our lives. I opened up to the man, sharing with him intimate details of my marriage. I told him we were practically estranged, and that Adam worked endlessly while I gallivanted around town trying to strike it rich. He listened so intently; I got carried away. The next thing I knew I was telling him how I was over my head in debt, desperate to find a way out before it was too late.

Larry took my hand, held it tenderly in his. I sobbed as I told him I wondered if my husband still loved me.

After deciding we did not want the evening to end so soon, we drove to where Larry was staying. We found the Video Lottery Terminals in the main floor lounge where, conveniently, two machines sat vacant side by side. So we played a while, leisurely pressing our spin buttons, exchanging an occasional word or two, likely something pertaining to our games—happy praise, intermingled with the occasional mild expletive no doubt.

After a time, Larry announced that he'd run out of money. He invited me to join him for a "harmless walk" up to his hotel room where he planned to dip into his "stash of cash." I'd known him for a little over six months at this point, and thus far, he'd been a perfect gentleman—for the most part, anyway. So I was not particularly concerned about my safety, and, surprisingly enough, although I'd gone months without physical intimacy with my husband and was now half way to the hotel room of a very attractive man, an affair of any shape or size was about the furthest thing from my mind. Perhaps in finding the temporary means to finance my gambling, the void in other departments of my life had been temporarily satiated.

Not a word was spoken en route to Larry's room. It seemed we were both lost in our own thoughts, and perhaps a little breathless from the ascent. After having sat for so long, we'd opted to take the stairs.

Larry flashed me a handsome smile as he slid the room card into the slot. I smiled back. He returned his attention to the task at hand, proceeding to open the door when the green light gave him permission to do so. As he closed the door, he asked if I minded him taking a quick shower, jokingly inviting me to join him.

I turned on the television set and made myself comfortable.

A pleasant aroma drifted out on the long wisps of steam, and as Larry emerged looking handsome and refreshed, I couldn't help but wonder how much he'd paid for the expensive-smelling cologne. He looked good in his blue jeans and golf shirt, the white fabric suggestively snug against his still moist skin.

I returned my attention to the task at hand—surfing over the vast selection of satellite channels the hotel had to offer. As Larry approached, I rose from the edge of the bed to stand next to the television cabinet. He brushed against me, *ever so slightly*, as he passed by, and then stopped before the night table at the far side of the bed. I returned to my seat, sinking down into the field of wheat and flowers to be nearly swallowed whole by the too-soft mattress below.

I heard the night table drawer being pulled out. Slowly, I turned to peer over my shoulder. I watched as Larry retrieved from the small space a thick wad of bills. My eyes grew bigger. The money was secured with a shiny gold money clip. *Probably real gold*, I decided.

As Larry rose to his feet, I turned my attention back to the television set. Retracing his steps, the man with the money returned to where I was seated. He stopped directly in front of the television, blocking my view of the screen. I opened my mouth to let him know he made a better door than a window, but no words came out.

Slowly, deliberately, he removed from the money the expensive-looking clip. My mind turned to mush as he fanned the wad of bills. It seemed to be happening in slow motion. I was almost certain I felt a feathery breeze at my face. It smelled like money. My skin turned to gooseflesh, my stomach filling with butterflies.

The entire time, Larry had avoided eye contact with me. It was as though he, too, were mesmerized by the fat wad of talented twenties and fifties dancing in the palm of his hand. Not yet changed into Canadian currency, the bills were less than colorful, yet they impressed me as though each contained a rainbow.

The show ended and Larry pulled several of the bills loose. He tucked them carefully into his wallet. For the first time, he peered down at me. Our eyes met and held. What felt like a very generous moment passed in which neither of us spoke. Then, in perfect unison, our eyes returned to the remaining money. I watched as Larry counted out three hundred dollars, mostly twenties, to place them in a neat pile beside me on the bed. He stood directly before me, the smallest of spaces between us. As he gazed down at me, my heart began to race. I could hear its strong, rhythmic beat at my ear, its persistent pulse at my temple. The palms of my hands grew moist.

And then I noticed something that took me by surprise. It was Larry's eyes—they were filled with compassion.

His voice soft and soothing, he said, "Joan, it seems to me you're having some financial difficulties and it's making you unhappy. I enjoy spending time with you and like nothing more than to see you smile. It would be an honor if you would allow me to help you out." I found his kindness overwhelming, but at the same time, intuition was telling me to be leery.

As nonchalantly as possible, I glanced at the three hundred dollars lying next to me. I did not want to appear eager. *Just in case.*

Immediately, my mind drifted off; I thought of the overdue bills and how nice it would be to have real food in the house; I imagined what a good night sleep might feel like. *All I have to do is reach out and take it...*

Tearing my eyes from the money, I replied, cautiously, "Larry, I appreciate your offer. If I accept, can we agree that it is just a loan and I will repay you as soon as I can?" I was determined to keep my (last shred of) dignity intact.

My heart began to pound like crazy as I awaited his reply and I was relieved when a small smile found his lips. "It's entirely up to you," he said. "But do take the money. We'll worry about the details later." Before I could wonder what the "details" might be about, he'd scooped up the three hundred dollars and placed them in my hand. I wanted to toss them into the air and let them rain down around me. I wanted to spread them over the bed and curl up in them. Instead, I tucked my newfound treasure into the small, zippered compartment of my purse. Out of sight, out of mind. Or so they say...

And then his arms were around me, his body pressing against mine, his warm breath whispering against my ear, "This is okay, isn't it?"

I did not respond.

Larry withdrew slightly, enough to bring his face before mine. I started to speak... He pressed his lips against mine. My body grew rigid. I wanted to freak out, yell at him. I wanted to shout in his face, "It's a wee bit early to be collecting interest, don't you think?!"

Slowly, I pulled away. Eyes downcast, I whispered, "I'm sorry. I... I just can't."

I could see the disappointment on his face, and was surprised a moment later when he said, simply, "Oh... Okay... Why don't we go back downstairs then?"

We sat at a small table in the mostly deserted lounge. Larry ordered himself a beer and a 7-Up for me. If he felt as uncomfortable as I did, he hid it well. I struggled to make conversation. His terse, one-word replies said it all.

Silence fell. I tried not to look at the slot machines. The grip on my purse tightened.

Finally, after what felt like forever, I said, "Larry, if you want the money back I will totally understand. You surprised me up there, that's all. Please talk to me." He was thoughtful a time, then replied, "Joan, I hope you don't think I was trying to buy your affections. I admit that I am attracted to you, but my intentions to help you are sincere. Guess I just got carried away. I apologize." I smiled, although I didn't feel much like smiling. "Apology accepted," I said. "Can we get past this?"

Apparently I must have gotten past it; by the end of the evening I'd provided Larry with my telephone number.

Larry would call each time he came to the city, and we'd meet up for a combined effort to apprehend the ever-elusive jackpots. It worked out well for me, what with Larry affording the money for the two of us to play and each of us splitting our winnings fifty-fifty. Larry was always luckier than I was.

Unfortunately, my share of the profits always seemed to disappear shortly after Larry disappeared. I was on an endless quest to win more, but regardless of how much I won, it was never enough. I chased after new money... I chased after old money... It was a lot like riding a merry-go-round of madness, really. 'Round and 'round and 'round I went, always ending up without a cent.

Stupid dizzy bitch.

A PLACE WHERE WEEDS & ROSES GROW

22

A Not-so Pretty Woman

My self-loathing became more acute with each passing day—especially on days filled with gambling. Mind you, the "days off" were anything but a reprieve. It took a great deal of time and energy to conceive and carry out a plan clever enough to finance a session at the slots, you see.

By now, my husband treated me as little more than a leper. Frankly, I didn't give a damn. I was either too tired to care, or too busy gambling—usually both. Besides, with the way I'd been taking care of myself, it would have come as little surprise to learn that I'd developed some god-awful disease. *Is there such thing as leprosy of the soul?* It would certainly explain the empty feeling I had growing inside of me...

My husband was drinking more and more now, and although a part of me was genuinely concerned for his wellbeing, another part of me was glad for it. Every now and then I would make a comment, like when I noticed him using Bailey's as a substitute for coffee cream in the morning, or when the beer and liquor bottles had piled up to the point where I was almost tripping over them. The more I mentioned his "little problem," the less he mentioned mine.

My struggle to maintain the household finances continued. Telephone bills had become astronomical with my excessive phone calls. All hours of the day and night I telephoned my parents, lamenting over my financial woes, concocting long, drawn-out stories to explain the latest crisis. Every once in a while it would pay off, but never often enough.

More often than not I managed to fend off utility disconnection notices only at the last possible minute. Food continued to be a rarity, and my husband had become a virtual stranger. Life was really beginning to suck.

The magnitude of my predicament became even more evident when I was forced to resort to shoplifting for bare necessities, such as deodorant. Considering the time I spent sweating in front of the old slot machine, it was one item I simply had to have.

Whenever I was out in public, I'd stare at women's purses, and have mini-fantasies about snatching one or two and then racing off to the nearest slot machine. My heart would pound so hard at my ears that all sound around me would become muted. I felt wretched and crazy and wished I could just vanish from the face of the earth.

I had to find a solution before I lost what little remained of my sanity.

An NSF cheque found its way into my personal chequing account this time. It was made payable to me and deposited into the account against which the cheque was written. Although this failed me miserably in my previous attempt with the business account, it could not possibly go awry a second time.

I snatched up the tidy sum of brand new, unblemished

bills dispensed by the automated teller machine and headed for my favorite gambling spot.

The VLT machines inflicted cruel and unusual punishment on me that day. No sooner had I given up on one machine to try my luck at another, would some SOB come moseying along to park his or her behind at my original machine and hit a substantial win. It seemed a great conspiracy was underway, with the sole objective being: Drive Joan crazy! And by day's end, it certainly seemed they had gotten their way.

Depression engulfed my entire being. I felt weighted down with hopelessness, my thoughts unfocused, nonsensical at best. Nothing seemed to help.

Oh, how I longed to escape my life. Perhaps I'd fly off to some enchanted island paradise, one entirely secluded with a warm tropical breeze and soft sandy beach, hypnotic ocean of sparkling blue to lull my tortured mind. Maybe I'd find Lewy there... Or maybe I'd return to Vegas where it all began... where the pretty colors and shapes were so much kinder...

Or maybe I'd take a trip to the bloody moon; surely my husband would provide me a one-way ticket.

That evening, Adam answered several annoying hang-up calls. As we happened to be occupying the same room of the house at the time, had I answered the telephone, Larry would have been immediately informed that he'd reached a wrong number.

Sleep came easier than usual that night, likely due to a sense of relief knowing I would see Larry the following day.

Saturday morning played out as usual with Adam chomping at the bit and heading out the door at eight o'clock sharp. The moment I saw his white work van turn the corner at the end of our street, I picked up the telephone.

Larry and I met for brunch, and by early afternoon we were cozied up side by side before two playful slot machines. Success was ours, but not nearly to the extent I so desperately needed. The only way I could possibly escape the impending wrath of the bank was to deposit the amount of the NSF cheque I had written prior to Monday morning. Even then I would likely have some explaining to do.

We walked outside to the parking lot and found my car, crawled inside to enjoy the fresh afternoon breeze flowing through the open windows. Larry dared to bring along his alcoholic beverage from the bar, while I sipped on my bottomless glass of 7-Up. We chatted about work and this and that while I secretly gathered the courage to tell him about my dilemma.

After exchanging idle chitchat for a half-hour or so, I decided it time to get down to business. But first, I would need a good, stiff drink.

Larry was surprised, as was the barmaid, when I requested a double shot of Vodka in my next 7-Up. So rarely did I consume alcohol that not only did it provide me some much-needed courage, but also, a three-inch thick tongue and pair of most unsteady legs.

Effortlessly, I presented the details of my predicament, highlighting my most recent blunder, which, I explained, teary-eyed, had left me in dire straits. As I finished my rambling confession, I half-expected the man to call me an idiot and get up and leave. But he didn't. Instead, he expressed sympathy for my troubles and asked me how much money I needed.

He did not bat an eye when I told him I needed five hundred dollars. I wished I'd asked for more.

As we passed by, Larry reached in and flicked the bathroom light switch on. He did not reach for the main switch as we continued into the hotel room.

I lowered myself onto the edge of the bed. Larry sat next to me. As the bedside lamp came to life, I watched Larry slowly withdraw his wallet from his pants' pocket to set it atop the night table. Our eyes met. I looked away. He reached for the lamp a second time; the soft, yellow light disappeared.

As my eyes adjusted to the sudden dimness, Larry got up from the bed. He walked over to the bathroom and, upon entering, pulled the door closed behind him. Near darkness enveloped me. I wished it would swallow me up entirely.

His feet fell so softly against the carpet that although I knew he was coming for me, I was startled nonetheless when he arrived.

He kissed me hard on the mouth. Momentarily, I returned his kiss, and then pulled away. I thought of *Pretty Woman*—the warning Kitt gave Vivian not to kiss on the lips... And then I thought about the silence. It was so quiet I could hear my heart beating at my ear again. Thump-*thump!* ... thump-*thump!*... thump-*thump!*...

We sat in the silent darkness for what felt like forever. I wondered if I should say something. But, what? I could think of nothing. I began to feel light-headed. I wondered if the bed was spinning like it used to when I was a teenager. It was too dark to tell. I wished I'd never had that drink.

The sound of Larry's voice startled me. "I can't recall the amount of money you said you needed. Was it five hundred?" Each syllable was uttered in monotone. It didn't even sound like him.

Although the voice was eerie and disturbing, it relayed the message loud and clear. I did not respond right away.

Everything was so surreal. My mind raced frantically, but got nowhere.

"That's right," I said, after God knows how long. I then excused myself and made my way to the washroom. My legs still felt like rubber.

I lowered myself onto the cold rim of the tub and hung my head. I needed a moment to think, clear my head. When I closed my eyes to search for answers, the quiet darkness reminded me of what was awaiting me in the other room. *What happened to the generous, fun-loving, no-strings-attached Larry?* I wondered.

I opened my eyes. I knew what I must do. It took every ounce of willpower, but I managed to not cry.

Upon opening the door, I turned off the light and stood in the doorway. I remained there a long, thoughtful moment, my hands bunched into fists at my sides. They felt warm, clammy. I shook them open. A deep breath and I forced my feet to move.

The faint silhouette of a man appeared in the darkness; I wished it were my imagination. A moment later, harsh reality confirmed it all too real.

Larry tugged at my clothing. I cringed. The next thing I know, my hands are wrapped around his wrists and I'm pushing him slowly, deliberately away from me. His torso suddenly stiffens; he refuses to budge another inch. Before he can say anything, my fingers find the small, rectangular piece of metal and lower the zipper to his jeans. Immediately, he sheds his shirt and trousers and stretches full-length over the bed. For a brief moment I wonder if he would give chase, stark naked, if I was to grab his wallet and run...

My spirit wept as I performed oral sex on the man, and I nearly vomited when he climaxed.

Returning to the washroom, I rinsed my mouth with scalding hot tap water. Then, after rummaging through the small, black travel case I'd taken mental note of earlier, I placed a large gob of toothpaste on the tip of my right index finger and proceeded to scrub my teeth and tongue until my entire mouth sizzled with mint. Again, I rinsed with water. Still, my mouth felt foul.

I shivered all the way home. Never in a million years could I have imagined that I would one day discover first-hand how a prostitute earns her money.

By now, the dogs rarely bothered to bark when I arrived home. More often than not, there was nothing for them to get excited about. They greeted me with a yawn and half-hearted wag of their tail, before heading out the back door to relieve themselves. I made my way to the washroom and turned on the light.

Reluctantly, I peered into the mirror. I did not expect it to be kind to me, as it seldom was in recent months (perhaps years), but this time it caught me by surprise. I hardly recognized myself. The worry lines that had been gradually building around my eyes were suddenly deep and very telling; I could practically see my latest sin there. And my once pretty, blue-green eyes appeared only sad and tired now. Perhaps I should not have been so surprised... After all, I now only looked on the outside as I'd been feeling on the inside for so very, very long.

I looked thinner than ever, which became only more apparent when I removed my clothing. My skin was paler than usual and looked so strange, as it was pulled taut over my every muscle and bone. I looked half starved.

The bathroom scale told me I'd lost weight. But I already knew that.

Stepping into the shower, I bowed my head to receive the crown of warm water; it was like a gift, my tears mingling with the gentle flow of liquid as though they never existed at all. And for a brief moment in time—for one incredibly beautiful, merciful moment—everything was okay...

...And then the moment was gone, and with every fiber of my being I prayed to God, pleading with him to wash away my shameful sins.

23

A Pocket Full of Betrayal

*A*m *I evil? Am I insane? Am I a whore? Will my husband ever love me again?* These are the kinds of questions that now kept me awake at night. The shadows at my ceiling told me Yes... Yes... Yes...and... Of course not! But sometimes the sun would come up and my demons would mercifully fade into the morning light, leaving behind a small glimmer of hope.

Oh, how I hated the cloudy days...

Every morning for a week I performed the same sexual favor for my husband as I had for the man in the hotel room. Although Adam seemed to enjoy the physical pleasure of the act, he did not suddenly grow any fonder of me.

It was the only physical contact we'd had in a very long time. Our relationship had become virtually non-existent. We rarely spoke, and when we did, our conversations consisted of his questions and accusations, accompanied by my lies and alibis. On the occasions when he'd care to inquire as to my whereabouts, I'd kindly suggest he spend more time with me and find out for himself. And when he'd demand to know the status of the household bills, I'd kindly suggest he go screw himself.

One day out of the blue I began nagging my husband to spend time with me. It had been forever and a day since I'd done that. I chastised him for not being affectionate, scolded him for being a workaholic and for drinking too much, and last but not least, accused him of having an affair.

Later that same day, as I was searching the house for something to light a cigarette, I noticed Adam's coat draped over the back of a chair. Just as I reached in to check the pocket, Adam appeared in the doorway. When he demanded to know just what the bleep I thought I was doing, I was, for the first time in a long time, able to answer his question truthfully—I told him I was looking for his lighter.

Without warning, Adam reached out and attempted to snatch the coat away. Seeing the panic in his eyes I instinctively grabbed hold of it, and a struggle ensued. The more determined he became, the harder I yanked on the coat.

A half-minute or so later, Adam released his grip. His face had taken on a reddish hue and in an eerily calm tone he said, "Fine. Go right ahead. *By all means,* Joan... Check my pockets."

So I did.

Certain to find a condom or some other sort of incriminating evidence, I became almost disappointed when my fingers fumbled across a piece of paper.

And then I understood...

"I knew it!" I blurted, pulling out the sordid love letter. I shot my husband a look of contempt as I unfolded the note, cleared my throat as though it was home to the world's largest frog. Another accusatory glance and I was ready. Lowering my eyes to the page, I began to read...

The first couple of words caught in my throat like two enormous toad turds:

Hi Larry.

It closed with my signature.

Larry would reward me with money by wire transfer whenever I faxed him a smutty letter. Although my hand felt filthy after writing each one, it was nothing compared to the physical encounters.

My personality had taken on the kind of characteristics I'd always considered repulsive in other people. I barely recognized myself. I'd become utterly miserable, full of self-loathing and self-pity. I was extremely irritable, with mood swings so severe PMS seemed a thing of the past. In fact, I'd become so dangerously underweight that it was not uncommon for me to miss my menstrual cycle altogether. Good thing, too. I could scarcely afford a box of tampons.

I felt as though I'd boarded an endless emotional roller coaster ride. Or better yet, an endless episode of manic depression. It was like climbing to the pinnacle of mania with the anticipation of each win, only to plummet wildly into depression with the ensuing loss.

I wallowed in self-pity, blaming everyone around me for the mess I was in: If my husband were more attentive, I would never have started gambling... If my friends weren't so damn gullible, I wouldn't be able to borrow money to gamble... If my parents had a brain between them, they wouldn't continually bail me out of my financial messes... If the stupid bank had better security measures in place, I would never have acquired credit card debt... and if God had made my life just a tad more goddamned exciting, I'd have had no friggin' need to gamble in the first place! But my biggest complaint was aimed at the gaming commission; if they weren't so greedy and ruthless, they would increase the odds on the slots and I wouldn't have a damn problem at all!

What the hell did I ever do to deserve such crap?

My poor dogs steered clear of me. Early on, the desperate pooches had developed the ability to distinguish which personality inhabited my body on any given day. And that, of course, was determined solely by whether my luck was up or down. They'd watch me for a time, sizing me up from a healthy distance, and then either approach me playfully or head for the hills. Lately, they'd concluded it was best to avoid me altogether.

My predicament was bleaker than ever. My credit card was useless, my entire paychecks disappeared within hours, and over and over like a recurring nightmare, overdue bills turned into disconnection notices. Sleep escaped me almost every night now, leaving me in a perpetual state of exhaustion and anxiety. My driving became erratic. I'd speed like a maniac to get to my gambling destinations, only to race home after losing to hide the overdue bills. My driving record began to look like one gigantic computer error.

One fine day after tragedy struck at the slots and I was racing home to hide the mail, I heard a siren. Peering into the rearview mirror, I was to discover directly behind me the flashing red and blue of a Police cruiser.

Officer Stoneface displayed not the slightest hint of a smile as he wrote up the ticket, sternly informing me that had I been traveling a mere ten kilometers faster, I would have doubled the speed limit and been awarded a Dangerous Driving Diploma.

Upon renewing the car registration shortly thereafter, my husband was not the least bit impressed to be faced with a bill to the tune of four hundred plus dollars for my traffic violation fines. Adam was even less enthused when our car insurance nearly tripled for a year.

I became quite an actress after being forced to play the role of a normal human being while at work, and anywhere else other than gambling establishments. In fact, I'd hid my true identity from friends and coworkers for so long that being myself was no longer an option. Nobody would have recognized me. Too embarrassed to admit his wife was a raving lunatic, my husband played along with the charade. Only when we were alone together would I remove my mask. Not that it made any difference to Adam; he despised my every character, *real or make-believe.*

Unexpected company annoyed me to no end. Not only did I have to jump into the role of happy hostess without rehearsal, but scramble about to hide anything unsightly that might be lurking around the house. After being confined indoors for hours on end, the dogs would often urinate and defecate in the house. Nor was it uncommon for dirty dishes to occupy every square inch of kitchen counter space, with the overflow finding its way into our living room to adorn the various pieces of furniture. The only reason mold did not form on the leftover food scraps, was because two hungry dogs would find every morsel before it had the chance. With their meal times being so erratic, what choice did they have?

Relentlessly, I complained to my husband that the house was falling apart. I couldn't understand why he'd look at me as though I'd lost my mind. Meanwhile, my life was falling apart. Pieces of it were strewn over the floor of every bar in the city; my sanity and dignity, stripped away piece by piece and left to rot at the feet of those cold metal monsters I'd come to know so well.

But all of this was about to change.

Just as soon as my luck changed...

24

A Skeleton Revisited

I'd almost given up all hope of redemption when, once again, a lifeline dangled before me. I was astonished really that I'd failed to think of it sooner. Congratulating myself on yet another brilliant idea, I began the arduous task of fine-tuning the plan. *Not one mistake could be made this time.*

Meticulously, I scratched out every detail on paper to present to my husband. Then, the moment he arrived home from work... I pounced.

Accustomed to financing my sideline sportswear venture, a request for money came as no surprise to Adam. Not yet able to establish sufficient credit (gee, I wonder why?), my business partner and I required cash to get the order going, later to be reimbursed by the client, who, unlike us, had thirty days to pay.

Although Adam's suspicions flew pretty much on "auto pilot" those days, the proposal proved convincing. It appeared entirely legitimate, complete with the name of the company placing the order, an itemized list of garments required, and, last but (certainly) not least, the amount of cash needed up front. I explained that, as usual, it would take a week or so for the order to arrive from the supplier, and payment terms for the customer were the standard net thirty days. Plenty enough time to secure the big win! Of course, I kept *that* part to myself...

My plan unfolded perfectly. Victory was swift and sweeter than ever. My winning streak allowed me to get caught up on all overdue bills, and I even had enough left over to pay off the loan for the imaginary hot water tank. On a roll, I decided to return Adam's money early. I simply explained that the customer had changed his mind at the last minute.

Feeling entirely optimistic, I lopped my credit card in half and stuffed it merrily into the wastebasket. Continuing on my spree, I called the bank, requesting that my name be removed as the secondary credit card holder. Lastly, I enjoyed the final conquest of destroying all the tempting checkbooks lying around the house.

As reward for my outstanding performance at work, I received a nice raise in pay. My marriage grew to the verge of blossoming, and the dogs could not have been more thrilled with the sudden outpouring of attention being lavished upon them. I even had energy to tackle the insurmountable task of cleaning the house. It gave me a great sense of accomplishment to pay bills on time, and I enjoyed spoiling my husband with decent, home-cooked meals.

Traces of my former personality began to resurface. It was wonderful to rediscover humor, to experience genuine laughter again, and to feel sadness and shed tears over a sappy movie instead of crying only in self-pity.

Life could not have been better.

The long forgotten voice of John Wellington penetrated my blissful reverie like a missile of dread, sending a tremor of fear straight through to my soul. My unsteady hand threatened to drop the telephone. I could feel the acid seeping into my stomach, searing my insides, burning, burning... Perhaps a small hint of the hellfire to come...

I sank into the sofa, my mind screaming *Ohhh... myyy... gawwd!* How could I help but dread the worst? Obviously a confrontation was about to ensue with my former employer bombarding me with questions and demanding explanation for the missing money.

My mind drifted to a time and place I'd hoped never to revisit. Old transgressions flooded my memory as though the devil himself had opened the dike. One after the other they came, washing over me as though they might never stop. My face reddened, although there was no one there to see it.

"How are you, Joan?" I heard a voice asking.

"Oh... John...Yeah... I'm uh... I'm fine," I replied faintly.

"Did I catch you napping? You sound a little out of it."

"Oh... uh... no. No, I'm fine." *Couldn't be better... unless I was dead...*

I tried hard to focus on John's next batch of words, but it was not easy. I did manage to get the gist of what he was saying. "...in the market for a home theater system... Kate reminded me... ...your husband... ...man for the job... ...thought we'd give you a dingle..."

During the time I provided home care for Kate, I'd invited her and her husband to visit the showroom at Adam's place of business for a home theater demonstration. It was most impressive. In fact, Adam had taken me there for one of our first dates. *The big screen... the surround-sound...*

definitely worthy of a spot on the Electronic Technician's *'Top Ten Playgrounds to Take That Special Someone.'*

Adam received a generous commission for any sale of video and audio equipment he made during *or after* hours. So, naturally, when I'd discovered the Wellington's to be avid television and movie watchers, I couldn't help but wonder if they'd like their viewing pleasure enhanced. This could easily have been achieved with a six-by-four foot screen and projector, complete with state-of-the-art surround-sound. Unfortunately, my employers hadn't quite gotten around to making the big purchase before I'd so abruptly departed.

Although John's voice had opened the floodgates to some most unpleasant memories, the murky waters quickly began to recede as I realized he was interested only in audio-video equipment. Breathing a sigh of relief, I thanked my former employer for his call, assuring him that Adam would put together some sort of a proposal and we would meet with them in a couple of days.

Adam pressed the doorbell and together we stood expectantly before the heavy oak door. It was mid-afternoon on Halloween day and although the sky displayed not a cloud, only a bright orange ball suspended before an infinite backdrop of blue, I felt chilled to the bone. My teeth began to chatter and as I raised a tissue to dab at my nose, I noticed a purplish hue about the knuckles of my right hand. When I wiped my nose with the tissue I experienced almost no sensation in my hand. *Well that's awfully weird* I told myself. Withdrawing my left hand from the warmth of my pants' pocket I proceeded to rub it vigorously against the colder one. Still, it remained ice-cold.

Adam, who'd apparently been watching all of this transpire, suddenly blurted, "What on earth is your problem!?" Teeth chattering like crazy, I said, "I...I don't know. I...I just feel so cold." He gave me one of his amazing bear hugs, and immediately I began to thaw out.

Soon, we began to wonder if the Wellingtons were even home. Adam pressed the doorbell a second time.

As we continued to wait, my mind decided to wander off, and before I knew it I was standing before a closed door wearing a "DO NOT DISTURB" sign around its knob. Naturally, without hesitation I reached out to take hold of the cold metal doorknob, but before I could think to twist it, the door flew wide open on its own. There on the floor of what appeared to be a closet were the skeletal remains of a human being. The bones were in a seated position, and were dressed in thick, gray cobwebs. I felt certain that it was looking at me with eyes that were no longer there... but what did I care?

"I know who you are and you're not the scariest one, you know," I told the stark white bones below. "There are all kinds of them. Have you met the guy with the halo? He looks harmless enough, but man, could he do me some damage! How come y'all ain't hangin' out in the same closet anyway? Antisocial? Guess we've all got our issues..."

Sure enough, upon closer inspection... the blue clue that I needed. Stooping over, I reached out and pulled loose the small, rectangular object clutched between bony thumb and forefinger. Although I was already certain, I took a deep breath, closed my eyes, and blew. Beneath the layer of dust and cobwebs, I found on the blue bankcard the two words I'd seen a hundred times... *Kathleen Wellington.* Although the revelation entirely expected, a pang of guilt found my heart just the same.

"Earth to Joan... Earth to Joan..." came Adam's voice, mercifully yanking me back to the Wellington's cold, cement doorstep. "What's with you? You're acting awfully strange."

Just taking an unpleasant stroll down memory lane... ran into someone who had a few bones to pick with me... I felt like laughing and throwing up at the same time.

"I don't feel well, that's all," I said aloud. "Can we go now? Obviously they've forgotten about us."

No sooner had we turned to head back to the car did the front door open. John grinned at me and then reached for Adam's hand, apologizing profusely for the long delay. I made an effort to smile at the man, although I'm sure it came out more as a grimace.

We sat around the oval-shaped dining table, surrounded by the same large bay windows I remembered. The windows jutted out over an immense deck obviously crafted with a view of the city in mind, and as I peered through the spotless glass, I easily recalled the enchanting night scenes of flickering lights that had always reminded me of a mirrored reflection of Heaven's twinkling stars.

Kate and I did a little catching up while the guys hit the brew and talked sports. It was nice to see my old friend again, but at the same time, her presence stirred up within me a lot of unresolved guilt and shame.

Eventually, the three of us made our way to the basement with Kate cradled in John's arms, unable to maneuver the staircase in her wheelchair. He'd always talked about getting her a ramp of some sort; guess he hadn't gotten around to it.

Leading the way, I made my descent, remembering to turn right at the bottom of the stairs. I remembered the room well; often I would spend my break time strolling on the treadmill, daydreaming out the window—an exact replica of the large bay windows above only on a slightly smaller scale. It was also a room ideally suited for a home theater. But as I continued to glance about the room, I was shocked to discover that they already had one. Completely at a loss, I turned to John and said, "I thought you told me you guys are interested in purchasing a theater, but here I see you already have one. What's up?" With that, John proceeded to explain that the entire system was a disaster, a gigantic lemon, and that they were in fact looking to replace it.

Adam surveyed the "gigantic lemon," adjusting a wire here and a wire there, poking and prodding at the control panel. Then, the moment he opened his mouth to confirm it indeed an oversized piece of sour fruit, lo and behold, a picture sprang to life on the screen! Everyone turned to Adam who suddenly looked as though he'd been sucking on a lemon...

"Well I'll be!" exclaimed John. "That hasn't happened for over two years! How the heck did you manage that, my friend?"

Adam smiled sheepishly, although deep down, I'm sure he was snarling like a big bad wolf. He then rattled off something in electronic lingo, leaving us all completely baffled.

"I just can't thank you enough," John said, gazing wide-eyed at the picture on the screen. "The colors couldn't be more alive. And the detail... extraordinary! Please. Tell me how much I owe you. You've saved me a huge pile of money; the least I can do is compensate you for your time." Adam politely declined the offer, although I'm sure it wasn't easy for him. I could see him straining to see my wristwatch. *Tick* tock... *Tick* tock... Just for fun, I crossed my arms.

Kate, who had been dead quiet up until now, suddenly spoke. "At least stay for a video, won't you?" Before either of us had a chance to reply, she'd sent John marching back upstairs to grab some chips and dip, beer and soda-pop. Although Adam was an avid fan of beer, and known also to dip a chip every now and again, he looked annoyed as all hell. And even more so, once he'd pried my arms apart... *Tick* tock...

"I'm sure we have a good one laying around here somewhere," Kate mumbled, as she leaned over the side of her wheelchair to rifle through a large wicker basket filled with videocassettes.

I could not recall the last time Adam and I spent a Saturday together. Not needing a second invitation, I quickly settled into the center of the camel-colored chesterfield. I beckoned Adam to join me. He had little choice, really, but to play nice and comply, as John had returned with the goodies and was now watching from close by. As my husband sank into the sofa next to me, I felt positively giddy. *Who needs a slot machine???*

A moment later, after popping the movie into the player, John lifted Kate out from her chair to place her in the vacant space beside me. He then managed to squeeze himself into the small space remaining next to his wife at the end of the couch opposite Adam.

Must have been *some kind of beer* John handed my husband, as the next thing I knew, I had a large, wonderfully warm hand planted on my leg! It felt positively dreamy, sending sensations through my body that I thought I'd never know again. With eyes glued straight before me, I remained perfectly still, fearing that if I made even the slightest of movements, he would realize the error of his ways and his hand would be gone for all eternity.

The picture emerged slightly out of focus, appearing to be a home movie of some sort. I wondered if Kate had made an error in her selection. But she made no effort to change it.

A woman was standing a short distance from the camera, examining her surroundings. A moment later, she looked directly at us, and then proceeded to walk in our direction until she appeared cartoon-like. I giggled at her enormous nose and shrunken body. Hunching even further forward, the woman began tapping at something with an anything-but-steady finger. Its tip was so close to the screen I could almost make out its identifying swirls. The quality of the picture was improving. Her eyes appeared bloodshot. *Is she stoned?* I wondered. *Maybe she's just tired*, I decided.

The woman continued the tapping motion for several seconds and then slowly withdrew her face from the camera until her posture was completely straightened. She then peered over her shoulder, in what I perceived to be a nervous fashion. I wondered who or what she might be looking for. She turned her face back around and reached forward again, only this time there was no tapping. As she retracted her arm, there appeared to be something clutched between her fingers.

And then the woman's face came into focus.

Before I could scream, I felt a tap at my shoulder. I

turned to see what Kate might want. But she wasn't there. At least not the Kate I knew. A long skeletal finger was poking at my shoulder. I opened my mouth to let out the scream, but no sound came forth.

The hinges of Kate's jawbones began to work, and with each word there came a stench like nothing I'd ever known. "Where's my bankcard, Joan?"

Before I could think to answer, the bony finger pointed toward the screen. "Why, there it is! Look Bitch! There it is!"

I looked back to the screen to find myself smiling at the money in my hand. Still grinning, I reached out to grab hold of the transaction printout. I glanced at the tidy sum remaining in the account. My smile broadened. Extending my hand one last time, I reached out to retrieve the pretty, blue bankcard that had made it all possible.

And then the bony finger was back, poking at my shoulder again, more urgently this time... It poked harder and faster, harder and faster, until finally... it found its way *inside* my shoulder. A spattering of warm liquid found my face. I wanted to wipe it away, but my arm wouldn't work. So I just sat there, watching... waiting... *in absolute horror* as Kate Wellington got her revenge.

"Am I the scariest now?" she asked.

The actual visit to the Wellingtons proved nothing like the nightmare, thank God. In fact, it was an altogether pleasant experience, although they never wound up purchasing a home theater after all.

25

Amateur Night at the Slots

When the franchising company I was employed with found itself in troubled waters, I began to wonder if I'd perhaps brought along some sort of contagion from the last ship I was on.

Mr. Falzony eagerly hopped aboard, determined to rescue our sinking vessel. The new CEO expressed immediate concern for the low morale plaguing our office, and vowed to turn our sourpuss frowns upside down. Our Friday night staff outing certainly accomplished this; the fun-filled evening of bowling and booby prize draws in the casino's bowling alley left the entire staff in good spirits. There was hope for us yet.

Late in the evening, after having relocated to the lounge for a round of drinks and storytelling, the last remaining party animals decided to try their luck at the slots. As I was being dragged kicking and screaming toward my old foes, suddenly I relented. I figured *what the heck... I've a measly twenty bucks in my wallet... What could possibly be the harm? And who knows... Maybe I'll even win something...*

Not wanting to let on that I was an old veteran at the slots, I haphazardly dropped in a coin or two every now and then and placed harmless bets on games I was unfamiliar with. No one seemed any the wiser.

A feeling of discontentment welled as the last of my credits disappeared without a win. As though hoping the money fairy might have happened by, I checked my wallet. No such luck.

It was awfully considerate of the Casino to have conveniently located a bank machine at every turn within the building; I practically tripped over one to land at another.

Armed with a fresh supply of crisp twenty-dollar bills, I began plotting my strategy, and before I was back to my stool, I had it all figured out. Discretely, I fed the bill slot several twenties, my spine tingling in anticipation. I could hardly wait to see the expression on everyone's face when my light began to flash; of course, I'd act all ditzy, as though I'd no clue whatsoever as to what was going on.

But my light remained dormant. The big win never came. There would be no exquisite red rose atop my machine tonight. Oh how I wanted to plow my fist into the face of that shitty, shitty machine! Instead, I shrugged my shoulders and let out a sigh of indifference. *Oh, well... there's always tomorrow...*

My dear friend, Dawn, whom I'd grown immensely fond of during our time working together, nearly drove me crazy that night. She hovered over me like a noisy helicopter, her propeller-lips blasting me with an unending whirlwind of insight into the realm of problem gambling. "Can you imagine spending your entire paycheck on gambling? It's true! People are doing it! I kid you not! What a bunch of freaking morons! Kids got no food... marriage breaking up... what seems to be the problem? They claim they can't stop. Do you buy that? If you keep putting money into that machine you won't be buying anything! Get it? I just made a joke!"

Had the noisy windbag not been so intoxicated, I might have feared she was onto me. But she was definitely as drunk as a skunk. I could tell by the way she hip-checked my stool and called me Bastard every time I tried to ignore her. But I got through it, thanks to a little thing called fantasy. Thrusting my friend's babbling head through the slot machine window was a lot like killing two (annoying) birds with one good shove.

The next morning found me in a vengeful mood. Not only was I pissed with myself for having fallen off the wagon after such a long stretch of abstinence, but also, furious with the slot machine that had pushed me. It had also robbed my bank account of every dollar I had so painstakingly saved over the last three months. The house insurance payment was due in a few days, the phone bill nearly overdue, and food was scarce. It had been my intention to tend to those things with the money I'd saved.

I lay in bed stewing over my predicament, sapped of any motivation to rise and face the day. I could not imagine asking Adam for help. I'd rather have chewed my arm off than to have jeopardized my newfound status of model wife. Three months without gambling... by golly, I was practically a saint! There had to be another way. Somehow, some way, I'd find the money to recapture my losses and get the bills paid.

I cursed at myself for canceling my credit card; cringed as I thought of the pile of checkbooks I'd destroyed.

Noon came and went... and then... Bingo!

I stood in line before the wicket, a trickle of perspiration at my back. I felt hot and sticky and wished I could just skip this part and hit the VLT's.

With small, furtive glances I surveyed my surroundings; security cameras hung in every corner, strategically positioned to capture every event from every angle; a man wearing a security uniform—*patron or employee...?* I couldn't tell; a woman with unkempt hair standing in line one row over, two small holes at the back of her faded T-shirt—*I hope she gets herself enough to buy some new clothes...*

A boisterous "NEXT!" startled me out of my wits. I'd been jumpy since the moment I'd arrived, and the robust woman with the big voice wasn't helping matters.

I stepped forward, slowly reaching into my purse as I did so. By the time I approached the wicket, I'd retrieved the shiny, black object from within.

After exchanging a few words with the cranky woman before me, I raised and aimed my patent leather wallet in her direction. Slapping it down onto the well-worn counter space between us, I unsnapped the flap to fish out my identification. I then slid it through the opening at the base of the Plexiglas.

The woman scrutinized my driver's license for what seemed like an hour before starting her well-rehearsed spiel about applying for a loan against my next paycheck. Everything sounded fine and dandy until the part about my credit having to be verified. I believe it was right about then that I apologized for wasting the woman's time, did an about-face, and marched on out the door. *Stupid cow,* I mumbled as I passed by the window.

I sat in my car before the pawnshop, desperately racking my brain for another idea. There had to be a way. I simply could not allow Adam to find out what I'd done. It had been forever since he'd looked at me with something that so closely resembled civility. I could not risk going back to those cold, scornful eyes that always left me chilled to the bone.

And then there it was: my last remaining hope... and just a phone call away...

Surely enough time had passed to heal my conscience since I last conned my mother, and was it not just a little, white lie if I requested a loan to pay bills and simply omitted the reason for falling so far behind?

As I heard my mother's angelic voice agreeing to help me, I breathed such a tremendous sigh of relief that I almost missed the part about her having to dip into her last remaining savings.

By the time the money arrived by wire transfer, miraculously, I'd won the battle over the urge to double the money prior to paying bills. Before I could change my mind, I made good on my promise, utilizing the money to get the household finances in order.

Realizing how close I'd come to regressing back to the old, miserable life I'd been living really frightened me. And with every ounce of willpower I could muster, I trudged through the next two, long months without dropping a single coin into a slot machine.

26

Weeds & Roses

One Friday afternoon at the office my friend and colleague, Dawn, or Helicopter-girl as I'd secretly dubbed her, shared with me her suspicions of an impending layoff. What a co-incidence, I told her; I, too, had noticed the large cloud of doom hovering over the office. Actually it had been there for some time; we were practically down to a skeleton crew after all. Although the nasty storm seemed to have abated in recent weeks, it didn't take a meteorologist to sense its imminent return.

Late that same afternoon, I had a strange encounter with Mr. Falzony, our CEO. It was shortly after my having noticed an unusual number of closed-door meetings. Our exchange was so fleeting that I perceived it as almost curt, and as my mind replayed it a moment later, I noticed immediately the lack of eye contact on his part. This was in complete contrast with the attentive gaze and friendly smile I'd grown so accustomed to. The hairs on the nape of my neck stood on end as intuition softly whispered something was awry...

I entered my Supervisor's office and took a seat. I could sense the tension in the air before a word was spoken. Edward sat stiffly in his chair, hands folded neatly atop the desk before him. I tried to read his face, find a sign of some sort; it appeared stern, but somehow gentle at the same time.

I could find nothing further. And then I noticed the arched eyebrow. I'd come to know that telltale sign well; whenever Mr. Vincent was troubled or stressed (or annoyed... *with me*) he donned that exact expression as though it were a mask he simply tossed on. I don't believe he was aware of it.

"The atmosphere is strange in the office," I commented, when it seemed we were at a standoff for words. "It almost feels as though someone is about to be let go."

Edward must have reorganized his entire desktop before meeting my gaze. "I am so sorry, Joan," he said.

After great assurances from the CEO and my supervisor that my dismissal was in no way a reflection of my job performance, but rather, just another unfortunate side effect of downsizing, I was handed my final paycheck. It included a generous severance package.

I retreated to my workstation to gather my personal effects. It took only a few sad farewells and it was done.

I felt lonesome on the trip home. I was really going to miss that place. Many of my work colleagues had become like family. They knew me as a happy, carefree person, always joking and laughing—supplying the office that much-needed relief from the everyday stresses of the business world. My workplace had been one of the few places where I could be my old self; like a refuge of sorts, where I could escape the immense pressures of the gambling world and be free from my unhappy home life... if only for a time.

Upon arriving home, I felt utterly lost. Who knew what the future might hold with my escape route having been suddenly barricaded?

I broke the news to my husband the moment he walked through the door, by handing him my larger than usual paycheck to ponder. He merely suggested I budget accordingly.

At last glance, the luminous red numerals of my bedside clock tell me it's two in the morning. I finally drift off to dreamland where everything is back to normal and I am seated in front of my computer at work. Someone is asking me a question... I peer back over my shoulder... It's the brunette with the short skirt..."Oh...yes... Yes, please," I tell her. "A 7-Up would be lovely. Thanks for asking."... I turn back to my computer... There's an exquisite, red rose lying on top... It begins to flash... Faster and faster and faster... My eyes fall to the screen... Five shiny, red sevens are peering back at me... They're smiling, and dancing! ... My credits are climbing, higher and higher and... Ohhh myyy gawwwd—I'm on a quadruple-quadruple bet!!!

Although I'd slept but a few hours, I awoke with boundless energy. I leapt out of bed and into the shower, and although it was early, there was no time to waste. Styling my hair proved to be quite a challenge, as I'd not taken the time to properly rinse out the conditioner. Oh well, the company with whom I planned to spend the day would likely not care if my hair were out of sorts.

My first spin was magical. Five yellow bells appeared in a perfect line, tolling in unison as if to say, "Welcome back, Sweetheart!" They weren't red sevens, nor did they arrive on a quadruple-quadruple bet; but seeing how such a bet existed only in dreamland, the bells on a double would do just fine. Two hundred fifty dollars—not a bad way to start the day.

I'd been the first to arrive, waiting in the parking lot

for the pub to open. The early bird in this case got dibs on the choicest machine, and apparently I'd selected just that. My winnings continued to grow. Within minutes, the other machines came to life also, the familiar fingers of regulars eagerly feeding their bill slots.

An almost tearful reunion ensued when two of the six players recognized me. For five long months I'd been out of the circuit, with the exception of the staff outing. But that hardly counted. This was my old stomping ground, a favorite spot I had frequented from the beginning.

We laughed and played and got reacquainted. I simply explained that after experiencing a string of bad luck, I'd decided to take some time off. Not too much of a stretch, really... The only thing I'd neglected to tell them was that the "string" was actually a rope, and plenty thick enough to hang myself.

Over the years I'd developed a kind of kinship with several other gamblers. Pretty much inevitable I suppose, after sharing so many emotional highs and lows—the glorious wins and unbearable losses that ultimately define the gambler in us all. Often we bared parts of our souls to one another—an effort I suppose, to rid our consciences of guilt, shame and remorse. It became a cleansing ritual of sorts, there in a dingy nightclub of all places. I think a lot of us considered it our safe haven. Not safe enough, however, to admit to the true extent of our defeats or the deeds committed during the more desperate times. Nevertheless, there was an emotional bond; one that perhaps ran deeper than any of us could have fathomed while being seated there in the low glow of our slot machines.

My slot machine continued with its outpouring of

generosity, my collection of redeemable win printouts growing ever thicker. I managed to tear myself away long enough to devour a plate of greasy chicken fingers and fries, washing it all down with a 7-Up of course. I did not take my eye off the slot machine the entire time. Sitting at close range, I was more than prepared to holler at anyone with impaired vision who might happen by and not notice the "RESERVED" sign propped up in plain view.

My winning streak continued throughout the afternoon. Although entirely enthralled with the flashing light and ever-increasing fortune it brought, I kept my eye on the time. At precisely five o'clock, I asked my friend seated next to me to guard my machine with her life as I made a quick trip home.

Although my husband's workday officially ended at five o'clock, he rarely took notice, but in the unlikely event that today was the day he did happen to notice, I wanted to avoid drawing suspicion at my absence. This was achieved by collecting the dogs and leaving a note announcing that we'd gone for a walk.

After corralling Missy and Oreo into the car, I headed back to the bar, darting in and out of the rush-hour traffic while expressing a little road rage along the way. It was to no avail. During my absence, an inconsiderate old buzzard had swooped in and landed at my slot machine. "Sorry, young lady," he squawked, with anything but regret in his voice. "You were gone for longer than ten minutes. You snooze, you lose."

My friend apologized profusely, not that it did me any good, but I began to feel better as I headed to the bar to redeem my earlier winnings. Sure enough, as the bartender counted out my small fortune, "...three-fifty... four... four-fifty... five..." the unpleasantness of the incident became but a distant memory.

Luck found Missy and Oreo that day as well, affording them a good, long romp at their favorite off-leash park.

I slept like a rock that night... a happy, lucky, rich rock. Good thing, too... I would need all the positive energy I could find for the next go-round...

My winning streak continued into the following day—on and on and on... like some unstoppable climax... Right up until the moment it died. Croaked so abruptly, in fact, that I must not have noticed; I kept slipping twenties into the bill slot and pressing the spin button as though my credits were still tick-tick-ticking their way up to Jackpot Heaven...

That night I returned to my former workplace. Once again I found myself seated within the tightly knit walls of my cubicle, only this time, after ordering my infamous drink with the fizz, as I turned back around to find that exciting slot machine having magically taken the place of my boring, old computer, I was to discover not the smiling red sevens from fantasyland, but rather, a very real-looking trio of skull-and-crossbones. They glowered at me; I stared back, my eyes unable to flee. A whimper escaped me, as piece by fleshy piece the bony figures were made whole. I watched in horror, as each appeared more and more familiar. They multiplied, covering the screen to wag their fingers at me; I could hear them telling me, "Tssk...tssk...tssk." I wanted to scream, but my voice wouldn't work.

And then I saw the blood... creeping down, down, down

like some ghastly red drapery to hide the faces of my family and friends. The man with the halo was the last to disappear. I was grateful to have been spared their scorn, but at the same time, was terrified to look up; I couldn't imagine what the source of the crimson curtain might be.

Why, it's the rose! My exquisite red rose! I breathed a sigh of relief. The horror show was over. I reached out to take the thorny gift in my hand. Its neck was broken. Gently, I surrounded the fragrant cluster of petals with my thumb and fingertips to ease it back together. Fresh droplets of blood seeped out from the wound at its neck. The small, fragile head fell to the floor. I closed my eyes and wept.

I felt a tickle at my feet. I giggled. Something slithered around my ankle. Before I had a chance to react, the weed had wound its way up to my thigh. As it slipped around my waist, I began to scream... but no sound emerged. The weed was at my throat, its cold, sinewy fingers suffocating my pleas for help. Before I knew it, I was surrounded in darkness. *Am I dead?* I wondered.

Turned out I wasn't, but as I lay there gasping for air, staring up at my unforgiving ceiling, I wished with all my heart and soul and mind that I were.

27

And Then Everything Changed

Except for the odd wedding or funeral, I'd long stopped going to church. I don't know exactly when I stopped; I just know that there came a point in my gambling career when I was just too darned busy on Sundays. Or maybe it was because I could no longer look at that large, wooden crucifix without being overwhelmed by guilt, shame and remorse.

Seeing how Sunday was no more a "day of rest" for my ambitious husband than any other day of the week, he was out the door by mid-morning, off to eke out yet another hard day's work. Of course, I followed suit a short time later, although *my* day's work would not be *nearly* so demanding. It was, after all, a fairly simple task to lift a finger to press the spin button of a VLT machine. It did, however, prove to be one of the most emotionally demanding experiences of my gambling career...

Like the unpopular kid at the playground, the one machine sat vacant, its complexion appearing drab through the clear glass window. I gazed around at the others; each appeared healthy with colors vibrant and alive. As my gaze returned to the outcast, my eyes filled with compassion. And then there came a voice, informing me that the machine had caused its own undoing; that the little tyke had a severe attitude problem, was unwilling to play fair, and had caused several playmates to burst into tears.

After some consideration, I decided to take on the challenge of teaching the misfit a lesson in social etiquette. But by late afternoon, *I* was close to tears. I'd spent a small fortune and then some trying to befriend my impossible new playmate. Had there been no witnesses present, I likely would have beaten the wee bastard within an inch of his miserable life.

I spent a brief time-out in the corner, sipping my usual 7-Up and scarfing down a bag of potato chips. A quick inventory told me I'd depleted about half my funds, including both severance pay and the previous day's winnings. This, of course, was entirely unacceptable. *The slot machine has to turn around sooner or later,* I reasoned. *It can't possibly gobble up so much money without eventually regurgitating something.*

Slowly, and with heartfelt prayer, I slid my last remaining twenty into the bill slot. I pleaded with God to perform a miracle, offering up a bargain in return:

Lord, Lord, if you will let me win back what I've lost and not a penny more, I will never, ever, EVER gamble again...

The last of my credits disappeared without any trace of a miracle.

I cursed God all the way home.

Reluctantly, I crawled out of bed the following morning, sapped of any energy I'd ever owned. I made my way to the bathroom where I peered into the mirror, only to wish I hadn't. The evidence of sleepless nights hung beneath my eyes—sad, haunted eyes that no longer reflected the light of my soul. They were merely windows now, like those of an old, abandoned building, marred with grime and sins from the past. I looked so worn. *What happened to me?*

My lungs were heavy, my throat raw, after chain-smoking a couple dozen cigarettes with the previous day's fiasco. My fingers were stained a dark cheesy color; I refused to look at my teeth. I could not remember the last time I'd visited a dentist.

I reheated some leftover coffee and sat at the table. Sipping the hot liquid, I pondered my predicament, amazed at the way things had turned out. *Where did the last six years go? What happened to my marriage? Why did my luck have to run out? Why did I have to press that very first spin button? Why couldn't I just win big enough...?*

I hardly noticed my tears until Missy and Oreo came to kiss them away. They peered at me expectantly with furry chins planted at my knees, large maple syrup eyes overflowing with compassion. I stroked their heads and shared with them the woes that had taken over my life. They listened intently, although neither offered any solution.

I borrowed money from a friend to get by for a short while, but I knew I had to come up with a long-term solution in a hurry. As far as my husband knew I had plenty enough money to last a good couple of months.

Nothing sprang to mind—nothing other than an elaborate disguise and daring bank heist, that is. "JACKPOT-JUNKIE APPREHENDED BY LOONIES," the headline would read. The story would detail the botched bank robbery, explaining how, "The alleged culprit, reportedly a female problem gambler, surprised the tellers when she demanded only rolls of loonies during the heist. As the woman attempted to flee the scene, the seams of her overstuffed sack gave way to the weight of the heavy one-dollar coins, spilling the entire contents at her feet. As her next footfall met up with a roll of loonies, she was sent reeling, arms and legs flailing in all directions. The woman fell to the floor, say witnesses, breaking her neck with a loud crunching sound as she landed in a contorted heap with dozens upon dozens of shiny, gold coins dancing around her head." The story would draw to a close with, "...all bets are on for leniency, as many feel the woman has suffered a fate far worse than prison—a life sentence as a quadriplegic." And finally, "Although the woman will never recover from her horrific injuries, some people consider the paralysis consuming her body a blessing in disguise; without the use of her hands, Joan has, at long last, overcome her addiction to VLT machines."

I laughed like a freaking lunatic. And then I cried like I'd never stop.

And then I had an idea.

I turned off the ignition and began racking my brains. I knew already how much I'd withdraw from the ATM, as my daily cash limit was a thousand dollars. I just needed a story to go with it and a moment or two to gather the nerve. *Should have been an old pro by now...*

As I began to slide my legs toward the open door, I felt the hesitation of the shirt on my back. It was warm and damp and clinging to the seat as though freshly paper-mâchéd there. The material at my armpits was no better. Obviously, I'd forgotten to put anti-perspirant on. I couldn't even get that right.

I knew that what I was about to do was wrong, but what choice did I have? As crazy as it may sound, facing the wrath of my husband seemed a lot worse than committing instabank fraud. I was much too tired for a fight.

With unsteady fingers I keyed in my personal account information, followed by the deposit amount, before slipping into the slot the envelope containing the one thousand invisible dollars. It felt almost sexual.

I made two consecutive withdrawals, each in the amount of five hundred dollars, as the machine dispensed only this much per transaction. I fondled the money all the way to the car.

My big plan was to place an actual thousand dollars in cash from my upcoming winnings into the account, thereby counteracting the false deposit I'd made. I would take care of this early the next day, leaving only the simple task of having to confess to the bank my asinine error. This, of course, would be painfully complex in nature (involving a stash of instabank envelopes I kept in my purse for convenience from which I'd inadvertently drawn the one in question rather than the one into which I'd so neatly tucked the actual cheque), including several dizzying circles, thereby leaving the listener so entirely perplexed that they would simply thank me for depositing the cash and absolve me of my mind-boggling transgression. If they'd happened to have asked why I'd chosen to deposit such a large amount of cash in the end, rather than the cheque to which I'd referred, I guess I'd have told them... my doggies ate it?

No worries. I felt confident that my plan would prove successful. And it did... Right up until the thousand dollars disappeared...

Along with my will to live.

Suicide became the new plan. The details were a bit fuzzy at first, but the more I reflected on my life and the mess I'd made of it, the clearer they became.

I wept as I thought of my marriage and the man who'd grown to despise me. I cursed myself as I recounted the lies I'd told my parents. I thought of my neglected dogs, and my friends, distant strangers now. Grief overwhelmed me. "Why, God? Why?" I asked. "What is this all about?" The silence made me angry. I cursed at him. And then I cried some more. I told him I was sorry. And then I cursed at him.

I wondered if God would forgive me for ending my life. I'd been taught that the taking of one's own life was wrong, that every life had been bought and paid for by Christ's death on the cross. But I also knew that God was a merciful God; surely he could see into my tortured soul and would understand... *Wouldn't he?* It was all so confusing.

Eventually the details came together, and with that came a sense of elation knowing that soon my misery would end.

Sleeping pills. I'd always said I'd use sleeping pills. Never could understand why anyone would leap from a tall building or dangle from the rafters. *Why not close your eyes and drift away...* An unopened bottle of sleeping pills in the medicine cabinet confirmed it.

But first I had some letters to write. It felt right, even though I knew it highly unlikely that anyone would care to hear from the likes of me. *Good riddance bitch... Rot in hell now, ya hear?* I wished I had money to put in each envelope.

I decided to write my husband's letter first, as he was the one I had hurt the most. I decided also that I did not want Adam to be the one to discover my dead body. He'd been through enough. So I thought I would tape the note I'd written him outside the locked bedroom door with a message in plain view advising him not to enter the room, but rather, to call whomever necessary to take care of removing my remains.

Missy and Oreo interrupted my thoughts. They must have heard my sobbing and muttering and, sensing something was terribly wrong, came to jump on the bed to be near me. They lay beside me, one on either side, nuzzling ever closer to lick away my tears. I caressed their heads, offered a few words of comfort.

As they gazed into my eyes, I began to wonder what fate might have in store for them. *Who will love you as I do? How long before you understand that I'm not coming back?* My thoughts drifted to my husband; *will he ever forgive me? Will the brief, happy memories of our early marriage be forever tarnished by my betrayals?* I thought of my parents, wondered if their hearts would ever mend. And then my thoughts turned selfish... *Am I going to be remembered as the idiot who died from compulsive gambling?* The love in my dogs' eyes told me no, but at the same time, suggested I stay put... just to be sure.

And as I continued to gaze into their eyes, I began to pray. I prayed like I'd never prayed before.

And then everything changed.

I believe with all my heart that it was the divine intervention of my Higher Power that saved me from ending my life that day, in the form of an innocent expression of love, made by two very special dogs.

28

A Raging Storm . . .
A Glimpse of a Rainbow

Early evening found me staring blankly at the television screen. I was completely void of emotion. I was too exhausted to worry and there was simply no tears left to cry. I barely noticed the dogs' boisterous announcement that my husband had arrived home from work.

We exchanged our usual curt hellos, and then, after rummaging through the cupboard... the refrigerator... and finally, the icebox, Adam would make his way to the opposite side of the television room to take a seat. I could smell the whiskey as he passed by; hear the ice cubes crackling and tinkling against the oversized glass.

Not another word was spoken as Adam focused on his drink, and I, the television, which might very well have been a blank wall for all I knew.

Moments later there began to unfold on the screen some kind of dark comedic skit. I was somehow pulled from my stupor to find some crazy-looking woman in a really bad wig portraying a poor unfortunate soul attempting suicide. The gist of it, if I recall correctly, was to demonstrate, in a most exaggerated fashion of course, the ridiculous emphasis women place on their hair. Under normal circumstances, I likely would have found it rather amusing; however, the very concept of "normal" eluded me as of late. Regardless, it somehow motivated me to relieve my conscience.

I approached my husband and knelt on the floor next to his chair. He looked down at me like an anteater might peer at an ant, if he weren't particularly hungry. His show of indifference was nothing new; yet it caused a twinge of sorrow just the same.

As Adam looked back to the television screen, I peered at him for a long, thoughtful moment. His temples were dotted with more gray now, and the worry lines around his eyes etched more deeply than I remembered. He looked tired and worn, much older than his thirty-four years. The strong odor of whiskey made me feel sad. *What have I done to you?*

It wasn't easy to gather the courage, but I knew it had to be done. A deep breath and the words came, and the more I talked the more I had to say and before I knew it, I'd told him everything. I even fessed up to my suicide plan, including every sordid detail leading up to the desperate notion.

An eerie silence ensued. Intuition told me it was the calm before the storm...

Adam flew into a rage like none I'd ever witnessed. His initial reaction of quiet shock exploded into a fury of obscenities intermingled with eerily calm questions. *"Fuuuck! Fuuuck! You stupid bitch! Fuuuck! Why, Joan, why? What were you thinking? Did we not just go through this? Please, Joan, explain it to me, won't you? Fuuuck!"* With each segment of ranting came projectile spittle; I made no attempt to wipe it away. Had he out and out spat on me, I doubt I'd have done any different. The least I could do is allow my husband to vent.

I felt sick to my stomach, faint. And then an inexplicable

calmness came over me. After agreeing with everything he'd just said, I told my husband that I did not expect to be bailed out this time, that I intended to tell the bank what I'd done and would face the consequences come what may. "Yeah...sure," he scoffed, in a tone that made me wince. "And I'm sure your scrawny ass will be most popular in prison."

"Yeah... well... Maybe that's what I need," I told him. "All I know is this has to stop. I can't live like this anymore. I'm going to get some help tomorrow."

His face inches from mine, Adam glared into my eyes and solemnly swore, "I will pay for this one... last... mistake. But it will be the last, Joan, because I swear to God, if there is a next time, I will let you rot in jail!"

Without doubt, I knew my husband had never been more serious about anything his entire life.

Amazing Grace

The following day was a Saturday, the first day of July, 2000. It could not have been a more perfect day to embark on a new journey. I remember the sun shining down on me. Having been wrapped up in my addiction for so long, it had been forever since I'd noticed such a thing so it really stood out in my mind. Perhaps God thought my first day of recovery an event worth spotlighting.

It began at precisely one-thirty in the afternoon. I walked into the room with mixed emotions, feeling afraid and apprehensive, and yet relieved and hopeful. My heart pounded so hard I could hear it in my ears. I selected a chair and sat down. Moments later, I changed seats. I fidgeted nervously, fearing for a time that I might be sick. I wondered where the washroom might be. And then a merciful distraction; a steady stream of people began to flow through the door. Soon, about fifteen (presumable) fellow addicts had gathered around the long, rectangular table. A woman with brown hair offered me a smile. I smiled back. My heart settled down to a more normal rhythm.

Glancing about the table, I couldn't help but notice that there appeared to be at least one individual from every walk of life, from the homeless to the "well to do."

A gentleman I'll call Arthur chaired the meeting. He

opened by extending to everyone an invitation to rise for a moment of silence, to think about what had brought us there and to remember those who were still out there suffering. He then offered me a warm welcome before leading the group into some readings.

I found the literature surprisingly relevant to my own experience. In fact, it pretty much described me and my behaviors to a tee. *How did they know?* I wondered.

I listened intently as an astonishingly accurate portrayal of the compulsive gambler was unveiled; every insidious detail, as though the writers of the little yellow book themselves had experienced it all firsthand...

I learned of tools to arrest my addiction and stop my destructive behaviors and in the weeks and months to come, learned to uncover and deal with the underlying issues that caused me to gamble compulsively in the first place. I was provided a support system to help me cope with the aftermath, a group of people who truly understood because they themselves had been there.

And then it was time for "sharing." During this segment of the meeting I listened, as various members shared their personal experiences—starting with an admission of being a compulsive gambler, accompanied by the amount of "clean" time they had (amount of time since they'd last placed a bet). Some members presented themselves as an open book, sharing the darkest moments of their gambling careers contrasted with the "secret" to their newly acquired abstinence—climbing the twelve steps to recovery. Some chose only to listen.

As I listened to their stories, my fear and anxiety began to subside. It became apparent to me that I was among people who not only *shared* my deep, dark secret, but people who had *lived* my deep, dark secret. I felt a connection, a sense of belonging. It surprised me, really. Less than an hour before, I had felt completely and utterly alone; abandoned—perhaps even by God. And then there I was, surrounded by a group of complete strangers I felt like I'd known forever (or at least for the past six years).

I felt the healing presence of God in that room. He was all around us, and he was in us. I could see him in some people's eyes; others seemed unaware of his closeness.

As I looked around at all the different kinds of people, I realized that we were all the same. Sure we *looked* different from one another, but somehow it was easy to just shed that outer layer, that unimportant superficial shell of clothing and makeup, ego and façade, that so often becomes a wall, and see the naked truth beneath. And even though that naked truth was a broken human being with a hole in their soul called addiction, each was gracious and beautiful and I was grateful to be in their midst. Might sound like one big Hallmark moment, but it was my moment and I will never forget it.

We adjourned for a much needed cigarette break, offsetting the toxic fumes with the fresh air of the outdoors. I listened as some of the members spoke even more candidly of their addictions (which, by the way, ranged from lottery tickets to blackjack with slot machines smack dab in the center). When asked what my "drug of choice" was, I admitted it to be the slot machines. With that, several people nodded their head, a few in perfect unison uttering, "Ahhh... The crack cocaine of gambling." We swapped a few horror stories before heading back to the room.

I had remained silent throughout the first half of the

meeting, still somewhat wary about baring my soul to an assembly of almost-strangers. But by the time I took my seat for the second half, courage had found me, and before I knew it I was saying, "Hi, I'm Joan... and I AM A COMPULSIVE GAMBLER."

I thank God for showing me to the door that day. That blessed portal represents for me both an exit from my wounded past and an entrance to my present place of healing. July 1, 2006 marked for me my sixth year free from gambling.

I think of the heart-warming hymn *Amazing Grace*, as I humbly thank my friends for helping to save a wretch like me. How powerful (and personal) the words, 'I once was lost but now am found... was blind but now I see.'

'It works if you work it!' This simple statement, joyfully exclaimed immediately following *The Serenity Prayer* at the close of the meeting, is profoundly true and in my opinion, sums up nicely the effectiveness of the twelve-step recovery program. I believe with every fiber of my being that the twelve steps are indeed capable of carrying any and all addicts out from the hellhole of their addiction—provided they are willing to 'work the program.' ('Working the program' calls for the individual to have faith in and follow the basic concepts of the Twelve-step Recovery and Unity Programs as set forth in the program literature.)

Seeing how "I Messages" are encouraged at meeting level and the offering of advice between members... *not-so-much*, I cannot in good conscience ignore this opportunity to sneak in a few unsolicited words of wisdom. I suppose these unsolicited words of wisdom could also be summed up nicely by merely making a small extension to the earlier noted statement. If I chose to do so, I imagine it would read something like this: It works if you work it... *and if you take every precaution when forming new relationships, until the fog of addiction has lifted and you are healthy enough to detect the predators in the program.*

Unfortunately, just as there are scoundrels lurking in churches, schools, computers, (and perhaps most sadly... in families) and any other place it seems where two or more people are gathered these days, there exists in the twelve-step program what I refer to as "predators." These individuals are often there for all the wrong reasons; some of which I am quite certain have no addiction at all other than their sick need to control another human being through manipulation and twisted mind games. They lie in wait under the guise of whatever addiction that particular program addresses only to prey upon the weak and vulnerable newcomer who more often than not is unable to see them coming until it is much too late.

Before I go any further, I would like to state *very emphatically* that my intention is *not to detract from the fine program that helped save my life, or to discredit in any way its many fine members who are there for the right reasons,* but rather, to share my experience in the hope of sparing other newcomers the unnecessary added misery that I underwent. It is difficult enough to recover from an insidious addiction without taking on an additional element of chaos...

As I was walking out the door after my very first meeting, the gentleman who had chaired the meeting kindly approached and handed me a piece of folded paper. It turned out to be a list of the various meetings held around the city. Immediately, I noticed that several were circled in pen. "Don't go to these ones," he advised. "There are some less than honorable individuals that frequent these meetings and it would be in your best interest to stay away from them." He did not elaborate, but did add something to the effect that, "As much as I would like to, the anonymity of the program prevents me from naming names."

So, I took his advice and avoided the circled meetings.

It was perhaps my fifth or sixth meeting when a male member approached and struck up a conversation with me the moment the meeting was adjourned. He was very nice and told me that he'd been in the program for several years and could really teach me a lot about it. We chatted for a while and he quoted some scripture and offered me many complimentary and comforting words. I really needed that. I was so lost and broken. My self-esteem had been whittled down to nothing, and with my marriage in shambles, I was feeling less than lovable to say the least.

We took our conversation outside so we could have a cigarette. There, we found other members huddled together in small groups, some smoking, and most drinking fresh coffee. (It is not uncommon for members to socialize in this manner immediately following a meeting. Many friendships are formed within the program. Not surprising, really; after all, who better to talk to than someone who truly understands you?)

We were two of the last to leave, so engrossed in our conversation that time just slipped away from us. I remember the last thing he said to me before I turned to walk away... "You can trust me you know... God wants me to help you."

I found myself thinking of him often. He was handsome and smart and spiritual and made me feel so special. So when the phone rang one evening soon after that wonderful first encounter, and I picked it up to hear his voice at the other end of the line... I was ecstatic!

He asked me a pile of questions about my life and I must say I found it incredibly flattering that this long-time member of the program was taking such an interest in me. Understandably so, my husband didn't particularly care to hear anything I had to say, so it was wonderful to suddenly have such an attentive ear. The man seemed to hang on my every word. I told him about my gambling, my family, and how my marriage was falling apart. When I told him that I liked to write, he jokingly suggested that I should go live with him... he had a nice house... and I could live happily ever after writing to my heart's content... I must admit, I was tempted to pack my bags right then and there! He continued on, asking me many personal questions, and although I'd only just met him, I decided it safe to open up to him. After all, he'd quoted scripture with such sincerity.

Towards the end of that first telephone conversation, when he invited me to join him for a game of pool, I cannot deny the fact that I clearly heard my conscience tell me *NO*. And so, as difficult as it was, I somehow managed to turn him down, explaining that I did not want to upset my husband any more than I already had.

Over the next few weeks our telephone conversations

grew longer and longer and more and more intimate, while the distance between my husband and I grew larger. We began to see each other outside of meetings, and I found it nearly impossible to concentrate on my recovery program. Morning, noon and night, he was all I could think about. My every thought seemed to be entangled around him. He'd become like an obsession... my new addiction, really. I wrote him love letters and gave him a painting, promising that one day soon I would leave my husband so that I could be with him completely.

And then it all began to unravel...

I started receiving telephone calls from old-timers (members with a considerable amount of time in the program) warning me about the member with whom I'd been keeping company. Thank goodness my new friend had forewarned me that this would happen! "They're all jealous of me... jealous of my successes in life and jealous of who knows what else... In all likelihood, one or more will try to sabotage our relationship. I hope you will see them for the jealous liars that they are."

Indeed I did! I scoffed at the notion of my new companion being some sort of "Thirteen-stepper" or "Predator"! *How dare they?!*

And then I heard a horror story or two...

I was confronted by a group of members who proceeded to inform me of several disturbing incidents where female newcomers had developed relationships with the same male member as I, most of which had ended in tragedy. One woman had allegedly committed suicide shortly after he'd broken off their relationship. Countless others were reported to have left the program before ever having recovered from their addiction.

At first I defended him. It was just too hard for me to accept that this "God-fearing," long-time member of the program who'd lavished me with kindness and affection and all the things I'd been so desperately needing could possibly be the villain they were portraying him to be—not to mention the fact that I was the "only woman he'd ever dated in the program."

But then, there came the women...

One after the other, phone call after phone call, each with her very own compelling story—stories that started out an awful lot like mine.

When I confronted the member with whom I'd been involved, he became very defensive, going so far as to accuse *me of being the one* who'd initiated the relationship, telling me that after *all of my relentless pursuing* he'd merely given in to temptation and regretted it wholeheartedly.

After returning the CD of love songs he'd given me in exchange for a painting I'd later given him, I tried my best to move forward.

I found it surprisingly difficult to get past what had happened. All of the (obsessive) romantic feelings I'd developed for the man were now intertwined with ones of anger and despair, leaving me to writhe in a whole new twisted mess of emotions. I'd barely begun to untangle the ones from the gambling...

So I did my best to avoid him, steering clear of the meetings he was known to frequent. But then, somewhere along the way, something snapped within me. I decided that nobody, especially a good-for-nothing, god-fraud nobody like him had the right to interfere with my recovery! Along with this feisty new attitude, there came a strong urge to confront my "issue" head-on.

But it was just too hard. I became a nervous wreck every time we were in a room together. The moment I saw him, the anxiety would well up and my heart would begin to palpitate so wildly I thought I would have a heart attack. An icy coldness would find my hands and feet, and every inch of my body would visibly tremble. I could hardly speak. In fact, more often than not, I would remain silent throughout the meeting, declining the opportunity to speak during "sharing time."

Thank God I sought outside help, learning in private therapy that I had undergone what is often referred to as "transference," a transferring of feelings (or in my case... my addiction) from one person or thing to another, usually to a person in a position of trust. Sometimes this actually occurs in therapy, where the patient transfers his or her feelings onto the therapist. Of course, the person in trust is expected to have enough integrity to swiftly remedy such an occurrence, and is *certainly not* expected to be the instigator. By some miracle, this revelation allowed me to survive the ordeal without relapsing into my addiction. I did, however, leave the fellowship for an extended period of time.

I must claim ownership for my part in what happened, so I openly admit to having made the mistake of not listening to my (woman's) intuition, to ignoring my moral compass when it was so emphatically pointing me in the opposite direction. And as for the "God stuff," I should have known better... *even the devil can quote scripture...*

So please... if you are headed into any type of recovery program or center... stick with persons of the same gender wherever possible, at least until the fog of addiction has lifted and you are able to see clearly and make sound decisions. Find a men's group or a women's group if possible. There is usually at least one of each in every city. Talk to people... Find out who is trustworthy and who is not. Listen to your intuition. We are all needy and vulnerable when we first walk through that door and not everyone on the other side is a saint...

I am in the process now of trying to get a warning placed in the "Little Yellow Book"—the most commonly used piece of program literature. Sadly, it is proving to be a bit of a challenge; however, I do remain hopeful that it will be taken care of in the very near future. I feel it absolutely essential (not to mention a moral obligation) to have every safety measure put in place to protect the newcomer. It seems only fitting, after all, to provide the safest possible environment in which to begin the healing process...

As I said earlier, it is not my intention to detract from the fine program that helped save my life or to discredit in any way its many fine members who are there for the right reasons, but rather, to share my experience in the hope of sparing other newcomers any unnecessary added misery.

RECOVERY IS A BEAUTIFUL THING

THE TWELVE STEPS LEADING TO RECOVERY...
A BEAUTIFUL THING

Collateral Damage

My road to recovery has not been an easy road to travel. It has been anything but easy to do an about-face and confront the endless trail of destruction left in my wake. Fragments of my life litter the entire way, shattered by my addiction, waiting to be collected and put back together. Some can never be salvaged.

My marriage did not survive. Too much damage had been done to an already fragile relationship. It was just too difficult to find our way to any semblance of hope for reconciliation. I remember asking my (ex) husband if he'd like to read my gambling story. His reply: "No, thanks. I lived it." I'd understood this for some time; however, hearing him say the actual words while witnessing that flash of pain in his eyes, penetrated my heart and made me realize just how much my addiction had hurt him. My heart will never forget. We've become good friends, thanks to the power of forgiveness.

There are many victims who need to be revived, as they lay injured at the roadside, run over by my betrayals. Morals tossed to the wayside need to be salvaged and debts the size of boulders still hinder my every step. Bordering the trail stands my own personal forest of tall trees bearing huge knots of lies that still need undoing.

It has been an ongoing process over the last six years to admit my wrongs to those I have harmed through my addiction, and to make amends as best I can. It is still ongoing today...

I have heard countless stories of parents leaving their children unattended in cars or home alone while visiting the bar or casino to gamble. Unfortunately, I do not find this hard to believe. Especially when I recall the sweet, innocent faces of my former Bingo partner's three young children...

Although I have no children, my two dogs suffered terribly as a result of my addiction. They are currently enjoying more walks than all of their eight legs combined can keep up with.

I do not regret my experience with compulsive gambling. It has helped shape me into the person I am today. My only regret is the pain it caused others.

I keep hearing people tossing out what seems to be an absurdly low figure when estimating the number of problem gamblers in Alberta. And if memory serves me correctly, this figure has not budged in years. How can this be? The population of Calgary alone has increased dramatically over the last half dozen or so years... *as have the number of VLT machines.* Was I included in this figure? And what about the countless addicts I met along the way, the ones who sat on either side of me, wallowing in the same "secret" pit of despair and denial as I? How could they (The Stat-makers) possibly have known that any of us were suffering with a gambling addiction, when none of us were ready or willing to accept it ourselves yet? And what about the Internet gamblers tucked away in the privacy of their homes? Personally, I cannot help but suspect that the actual number of compulsive gambling addicts in Alberta is close to twenty percent, with the vast majority being addicted to the VLT machines. Almost everyone, to whom my mother mentions that her daughter is writing a book about her experience with compulsive gambling, eagerly responds with, "Let me know the moment it comes out... My nephew (or son, daughter, husband, wife, friend, cousin, aunt, uncle, neighbor, teacher, preacher, dentist, proctologist...) has a gambling problem."

I wonder what the "Collateral Damage" statistics would look like if the general population of Alberta were to be polled (or any region where gambling is easily accessible). If only half of the men, women and children who have been directly or indirectly affected by a loved one's gambling addiction were to participate... *I think we would all be profoundly shocked.*

Mr. Ed Looney, Executive Director, The Council on Compulsive Gambling of NJ Inc. (CCGC), was so kind as to provide me the following statistical information, and I quote:

The Council uses the 80-15-5 rule. 80% are social gamblers, 15% have a significant problem and 5% are pathological (compulsive) gamblers. Also, the addiction rate for adolescents appears to be a minimum of twice that of the adult population and studies in States and Councils appear to support that—New Jersey, New York, Connecticut, Detroit, Windsor Ontario, etc. We have for the past four years on our Website asked the Twenty Questions of Gamblers Anonymous, using the results to develop many statistics for adolescents from 18—19—25 and other groups. Also on the Website (www.800gambler.org), you can see an article I wrote, "Soul of the Compulsive Gambler," which offers further insight into the nature of compulsive gambling.

Mr. Rick Benson, Director, Algamus Recovery Centers, FL, offered the following information, and I quote:

"The researchers here in the States tend to "sub-type" the percentages into two categories—problem gamblers and pathological gamblers. I tend to use a gambling addiction figure of 5% nationally in media appearances. However, with significant "firing line" experience during the years of VLT legalization in South Carolina, the percentage felt like at least 15% as the Gamblers Anonymous meeting attendance exploded throughout SC and neighboring states. The machines were deemed illegal and removed in 2000."

Faith Interrupted

As my addiction grew progressively worse, so, too, did my relationship with God. My once ever-deepening faith (or, perhaps more accurately, ever-ebbing-and-flowing faith) fast evaporated into thin air until finally, there remained little more than a shallow puddle of insincerity. All of the good stuff, the love I had for self, God, and my fellow human being, had somehow turned to self-loathing and condemnation of everyone around me, especially my Creator. *Why did you make me this way? Why are you doing this to me? Why won't you rescue me?*

I came to offer him praise only after a win at the slots, and prayed only in desperation as my last few credits dwindled away. Oh, and sometimes in the wee hours of morning, as I lay alone with my tortured soul, I might have whispered a few words in his direction... *Please help me.* Or, perhaps more accurately... Please help me *win...*

Why did I bother to pray at all, while immersed in so much iniquity and hopelessness? When my every word seemed to fall on deaf ears? I really can't say for sure. Out of habit, perhaps (I know that sounds awful). Or maybe I was so lonesome and afraid in those moments that I simply had to talk to someone (not much better, I know). Like I said ... *a shallow puddle of insincerity...*

I remember for a time—I believe it was just after I'd committed insurance fraud—thinking that at any moment God would perform a miracle and snatch me up from the path of self-destruction I was on. Or, perhaps more honestly, I hoped he would grant the miracle I most longed for: The BIG WIN... the one that would single-handedly wipe out my every problem from here to eternity. I kept thinking, *You delivered me from manic depression, Lord... Surely you will save me from this wretched thing that has taken over my life...*

But he didn't.

At least not yet...

Perhaps I needed to experience my addiction more fully so I could write this book. Perhaps I needed to "Let go and let God," to truly surrender, but just wasn't ready (or willing) to do so until the time was 'right' (for me).

I would like to think that I continued to pray because I am (and was) at the core of my being a good and faithful child of God. Or maybe my continuing to pray had something to do with that deep-rooted longing for the (ultimate) "better life;" only mine was exaggerated, or intensified, during those brief, mysterious moments in which my gambling addiction kindly made room for thoughts of something else... Maybe I figured my only remaining hope for salvation and Heaven involved keeping that line of communication open. Or maybe... just maybe... it was simply a matter of *faith*... You know, that extra special kind that has people *leaping all over the place*...

Perhaps it was a combination of all of these things.

Or was it something my finite mind simply cannot grasp?

All I know for certain is that I needed to pray.

No matter how bad things got, I still felt the presence of my God somewhere deep within me. I honestly cannot say whether it was an actual physical sensing made of my own conscious intellectual design, or if it was a faith-based "knowing", emanating from some intrinsic part of my being, or soul. *Or was it simply a notion borrowed from the archives, from somewhere in the deep recesses of childhood teachings?*

In retrospect, through my much clearer vision today, I see that God was always there, completely and fully, regardless of the how's or why's. The details are not so important to me, but rather, the beautiful fact that he stayed with me no matter what... loving me when I was most unlovable. God never left me... I simply turned away from him for a time.

Today, right now, in this very moment, as I gaze up at the crucifix above my computer, I am filled neither with childhood sadness nor grown-up guilt, shame and remorse... *My heart is too busy overflowing with gratitude.*

32

The Blame Game

So? What have you decided? Is it my father's fault? Did he push his young daughter's small, fragile psyche over the edge the day he dared her to jump off that high diving board? I had one counselor who rather thought so.

Or how about my mother? She never did "get me." Kinda hard to appreciate a little girl who pees in her pants only to offer up a smelly demon-snake in atonement.

Perhaps my birth parents are off their rocker...

Or maybe it wasn't a family member at all. How about the abusive boyfriend? Perhaps something was jarred loose while he was floggin' my noggin. Plausible. Or what about that ex-husband of mine? Studies have proven that even baby animals do not fair well without affection, you know.

Drugs? Fried too many brain-cells? Or how about demon possession? That's it! The devil made me do it! *Certainly would explain all of my ungodly behaviors...*

Personally, I try to point a finger at no one but myself; the same finger, in fact, that I opted to use to press the spin button of a thousand slot machines. Early on in my recovery I made the decision not to play the blame game. If it were someone else's fault, I'd have had no reason to dig within myself to find the root of the problem. That made no sense to me. I had listened to enough fellow addicts and watched enough Dr. Phil shows to understand that addiction is merely the effect, or symptom, of a deeper, underlying cause.

Take a moment, if you will, to return with me now to my nightmare, the one where the exquisite red rose represents the flashing red light of a slot machine, and the weed at my throat, the ruthless nature of the compulsive gambling addiction... There have been countless times in my recovery where I'd gladly have been poked full of holes by thorns or strangled half to death by a weed, rather than having to have faced the aftermath of my addiction. *The consequences are endless...*

I'll never forget the day my big, black cloud of addiction began to dissipate and my conscience no longer had a place to hide. I'd never been so terrified in all my life. And it got a whole lot worse before it got better. But I survived. *By the grace of God, I have not placed a bet for six glorious years.*

To this day, I still suffer the effects of my addiction. Not only did it devastate me financially, but emotionally and spiritually as well. It took some time, but eventually I came to realize that God has forgiven me. Only then was I able to forgive myself and allow real healing to begin. As Pastor Wayne Lewry, a recovering addict himself, often says, 'God loves us just where we are. He also loves us enough not to leave us there.' I like that; it restores my hope and at the same time, reminds me that no matter the size of my sin, my Lord will gladly carry me beyond it...

Wandering aimlessly about in the darkness without my soul... I can think of no better way to describe my experience with compulsive gambling. I felt so lost and empty.

Can a soul detach itself from a living person? I don't know that it's possible, but what I do know is that the day I stopped gambling it sure felt as though I'd just been reunited with my long lost soul. Getting into recovery was like doing an about-face after having turned my back on God for an excruciatingly long period of time; it was so wonderful to feel the warmth of his light again after dwelling in that dark world of seedy bars and VLT's for six years.

What a relief it was to discover that God had never abandoned me; after all I had done, after all the rotten, despicable things I had said to him, there he was waiting for me... There he was still with me. *Hallelujah.*

It has been a most humbling experience to face those who I have harmed. I am blessed to have such forgiving and understanding friends, and my family... what can I say about my family...? Truly, they have shown me what unconditional love is. I didn't think human beings were capable of such a thing —until I was on the receiving end. Just as God was they were always there, loving me when I was most unlovable. Was it "by chance" that I was adopted into this particular family? I think not.

I'm both saddened and grateful when I hear of fellow addicts who have been abandoned by their families. I can't imagine. It is sometimes too difficult for family members and friends to forgive, thereby leaving the addict to fend for him or herself. Without the love and understanding of support groups, surely they would not survive.

I no longer gamble in any way, shape or form—not even lottery tickets. Although it was the VLT machines at the core of my addiction, I do not wish to tempt "fate" any further. When I keep my feet planted firmly on the ground (not so firmly as to prevent me from putting one foot in front of the other!), I find that my head stays out of the clouds where it is far too easy for me to begin fantasizing about the "big win"... A one-dollar lottery ticket turns into ten dollars... or fifty... or a hundred... How would it make me feel? Would it make me feel lucky enough to go out and press the spin button on a VLT just one more time...?

I don't want to know.

My journey into recovery has been a less than graceful one. I have succumbed to personality clashes at my recovery meetings... had bouts with complacency, both short and long, where I'd suddenly decide I was entirely self-sufficient thank you very much, bye-bye... and once abandoned the fellowship almost permanently to wallow in self-pity and bitterness after a hurtful experience with a male member. Thank God I had an extended support network to fall back on during that time. I journeyed for a while with a smaller 12-step group called FREED, and leaned more heavily on family, friends and God.

I've come to realize that it's no longer all about me; I was given tools to cope, and after a while, when I got "good" at using those tools, it became more about giving back. There's always going to be the new member, the broken down soul who comes stumbling through the door looking for hope, desperate to draw from the older member's experience and strength—just as I did, July 1, 2000... So I have returned to my original recovery fellowship, and while I'm there today offering my experience and strength to the newcomer, that person in return, without even knowing it, serves as a reminder of where I myself have so recently come. Yep... peering into the face of the newcomer is an awful lot like looking into a mirror of my never-too-distant past. *I must never forget...*

Many people call it "Self-help." Although my book falls into this "category" and is labeled as such, I'm not entirely convinced that this term applies to my own experience. I was, after all, led to the door of my recovery program by my Higher Power, Jesus Christ, and it was only after truly surrendering and asking him for help that I was to make it over the threshold. And it was there, on the other side of that door, where I met that roomful of people who so graciously shared with me their experience, strength and hope that I might one day find peace again. A therapist was instrumental in helping me to regain my lost dignity, and the love of family and friends, like healing balm to my broken heart and spirit. What was the "Self" part exactly? *Savoring Every Little Favor? Sponging (up) Each Loving Friend?* Hmmm...

Since the day I stopped gambling, I have made a concerted effort to fill the void that was left behind. This is really important for me. I stuff it full of good things like God, family and friends, and after long walks with my dogs I write poetry and stories until my hand is so gosh-darned tired it couldn't possibly want to reach out and touch a slot machine... It works well for me.

The need to escape my life seldom plagues me now. I like my life, and even when I don't, in those rare moments when someone or something manages to intrude on my serenity... I can deal with it! I reach out to a friend or family member, attend a meeting or two, or I use this amazing gift from God and pick up a pen and write about it. Or better yet... I find "escape" in a meadow of lush, green grass and wildflowers, far removed from the hustle and bustle of 'life', where there's only God and me and my two best friends, their black, velvety ears billowing in the wind... where the weeds at my feet are no longer menacing, no longer reaching up to stifle my pleas for help.

The nightmares have ended; both the real, and the imagined.

If you, or someone you know, is suffering with a gambling problem, know that you are not alone. Countless individuals suffer along with you. There is help available. I am living proof that recovery from this painful, insidious addiction is possible. If I can do it, so can you. With determination and support the compulsive gambling addiction can be arrested and the addict's life restored.

If you suspect you have a problem, please, decide today to make your last bet your last bet. Put your hands in your pockets and leave them there if you have to. Dial for help with your toes—or your nose if you're feeling extra tricky. Seriously... *Do whatever it takes.*

I won't lie to you—IT IS NOT EASY. But know this: Sometimes the life of a recovering addict turns out stronger, better and more meaningful than ever before. I know mine did.

It's so worth it.
And it's so entirely up to you...

Resources

AVENTA ADDICTION TREATMENT FOR WOMEN
Offering women with alcohol, drug and gambling addictions the opportunity for a healthy life and a new direction through treatment, education and support since 1971.

610-25th Avenue SW
Calgary, AB   T2S 0L6
Phone: (403) 245-9050
Fax: (403) 245-9485
Website: www.aventa.org
E-mail: info@aventa.org

ALGAMUS RECOVERY CENTERS
Founded in 1992, Algamus provides, through its recovery centers, gambling specific, residential treatment and transitional living for problem/pathological gamblers.

Phone: (800) 818-4491
         (941) 778-2496
Website: www.algamus.com
E-mail: algamus@aol.com

For information about **AADAC** (Alberta Alcohol & Drug Abuse Commission), which offers help for compulsive gambling:

Call their Help Line (24 hr) Toll Free 1-866-332-2322,
Or visit www.aadac.com

For information about **GAMBLERS ANONYMOUS** consult your local telephone directory or contact:

Gamblers Anonymous
International Service Office
Post Office Box 17173
Los Angeles, CA 90017
Phone: (213) 386-8789
Fax: (213) 386-0030
Website: www.gamblersanonymous.org
E-mail: isomain@gamblersanonymous.org

CELEBRATE RECOVERY is a spiritual, Christ-centered recovery program that embraces individuals suffering with every type of addiction. Celebrate Recovery's "Road to Recovery" is paved with eight Recovery Principles based on the BEATITUDES. The program was founded by Pastor John Baker fifteen years ago, and Celebrate Recovery helps with all 'hurts, habits and hang-ups'. This popular, fast-growing program comes highly recommended by Spiritual Leader, Rick Warren, founding Pastor of Saddleback Church in Lake Forest, California and author of the best-selling book "The Purpose Driven Life".

www.celebraterecovery.com

The **NATIONAL COUNCIL ON PROBLEM GAMBLING**
Washington DC
Website www.ncpgambling.org
E-mail: ncpg@ncpgambling.org
Toll free (800) 522-4700
24 Hour Confidential National Helpline

What is *PROBLEM GAMBLING*...

Problem Gambling is a gambling behavior, which causes disruptions in any major area of life: psychological, physical, social or vocational. The term *Problem Gambling* includes, but is not limited to, the condition known as "Pathological" or "Compulsive" Gambling, a progressive addiction characterized by increasing preoccupation with gambling, a need to bet more money more frequently, restlessness or irritability when attempting to stop, "chasing" losses, and loss of control manifested by continuation of the gambling behavior in spite of mounting, serious, negative consequences.

NCPG Mission

The Mission of the National Council on Problem Gambling is to increase public awareness of pathological gambling, ensure the widespread availability of treatment for problem gamblers and their families, and to encourage research and programs for prevention and education.

Additional Sources of Information:

www.abgaminginstitute.ualberta.ca

www.thechase.ca

www.femalegamblers.org

www.800gambler.org

Celebrate Life Recovery Service

Sundays at 6:00 p.m.

Every Sunday night at Central, a diverse group gathers in the sanctuary for *worship with a difference!* People in suits share a pew with bikers—the pastor wears shorts and sits on a stool —the worship band's name is "The Cracked Pots" and features pianist Guy Plecash (who is likely to break into a wild rendition of a hymn you *thought* you knew). And everyone feels comfortable getting a cup of coffee during the service.

Sometimes called "a meeting with music", the evening service is a SAFE place for people from all walks of life to come and hear the good news that Jesus loves them presented in a relaxed, non-threatening way.

Everyone is welcome—come on down and hear the good news in a fresh, new way!

Children meet downstairs in the Serenity Room, a.k.a. Meeting Room Two, during the evening service.

Located in the heart of downtown Calgary, Alberta, Central Church is on the corner of 7th Avenue and 1st Street SW. We are across the road from the Hudson's Bay and right on the C-Train tracks.

I find this group of people warm and welcoming, humble and helpful, and never judgmental. Also, they are a lot of fun to worship with! I find the Pastors' messages meaningful, sincere, and always relevant and inspiring to my recovery/ spiritual journey. If you are broken and in need of healing, or if you simply want to celebrate your faith in God with a great bunch of people, *Celebrate Life Recovery* is definitely worth checking out.

To those I have harmed, please know that my heart aches with regret. Seldom does a day pass without sad reflection.

To those who have shown me mercy and forgiveness, know that my heart sings with gratitude. Seldom does a day pass without joyful reflection. A truly remarkable gift, this forgiveness... One day at a time for six glorious years it has provided me the much needed courage and strength to live my life free of gambling.

What begins as a little harmless, recreational fun quickly escalates into a full-blown addiction, an addiction so severe that morals are tossed to the wayside and a crime spree is unleashed to support it. Before she knows it the woman's mirror reflects a stranger; she appears weary and worn, broken, and without hope. How ever will she escape to tell her story, to warn others of the danger lurking there?

She sees a door...

The Door

Addiction cast its spell on me
I surrendered to its charm
Heedless of my destiny
A future filled with harm
Tortured by my endless lies
My soul was filled with shame
Hardly did I recognize
The wretch I soon became
My resting place was soakin'
With tears from dusk 'til dawn
My spirit had been broken
All hopes and dreams were gone
'Twas in my final hour
I made a desperate plea
My Lord, my Higher Power
Please set this captive free
The shackles on my soul
I felt them fall away
God willed to make me whole
He healed me on that day
His gentle hand extended
And there I placed my own
Addiction's reign had ended
A seed of hope was sown
He led me through The Door
And there I saw your face
I could not ask for more
God's amazing grace

~Joan S.

From My Heart

I dedicate this book to my army of angels and its leader: My enduring parents, sister, and ex-husband; three very dear friends, George, Dawn and Lori; my therapist, Anne (now retired); my support groups, in particular, Cindy S. and Darlene T.; and above all (pun intended... sorry!), my higher power, Jesus Christ. Thank you all for your unconditional love and support and for so fiercely fighting to save my soul.

Thanks, Dad, for being my source of strength. I'll never forget the loving embrace you gave me when I revealed my shameful secret; and Mom, I'm so glad you suggested I keep a journal of my journey into recovery, which ultimately led to this book. Thank you for shedding as many tears as I did. Thank you both for your compassion, forgiveness, and encouragement.

And I'm grateful to you my sweet sister (never thought I'd use those two words in the same sentence!). I fondly recall your inspirational words of praise as dad read aloud my journal when introducing my addiction, "That's really good, Joan!" It encouraged me to unfold my experience in its entirety onto the pages of this book. Thank you for that.

To the husband I have lost—thank you for your countless efforts to rescue me. How you must have suffered. How amazing is your heart to have forgiven me...

And to Dawn, my dear (Helicopter-girl) friend, who discovered my addiction through reading the very first draft of this story... Thank you for being there for me, for being my soft place to fall. I miss you...

To my lifelong friend, Lori—thank you for your unconditional love, countless words of encouragement and many prayers. I'm blessed to know you, blessed to have discovered so early in life the amazing spirit that resides just beneath that kooky façade of yours. Don't ever stop being you!

George, from the bottom of my heart I thank you. I'll never forget the moment I told you about my gambling problem. It would have been so easy for you to have judged and condemned me, but instead, you said, simply, "How can I help you?" You have been a tremendous source of support in so many ways. Without your help it would have been a near impossible task to bring this story to completion.

And Anne McFaul, therapist and friend—thank you for helping me to reclaim my dignity.

Margaret... Thank you for taking me under your (dragonfly) wing and for teaching me so much. You have an extraordinarily generous heart. And I am so glad you introduced me to Sandra...

To my publisher, Sandra Janssen of Windshift Press—thank you for recognizing the importance of my story and for helping to bring it to the forefront. I especially appreciate the respectful manner in which you handled this sensitive issue. Happy dancing...

And last but certainly not least, a special thanks to my editor, Darrin Smyth. Your thorough, light-handed touch with the marking pen during the editing process (along with your fun personality!) helped make this "segment" of my journey a most pleasurable one.

For each and every one of you, I am grateful to God. Your love is the luminous light that led me out from the dark place of addiction; the same glorious light that continues to shine today, providing me some much needed hope on this long and winding road called *Recovery*.

~Thank you for reading my story~

My hope for you and your loved ones:
a long and fruitful life...
May your every day be filled with God's blessings—
faith, hope and love,
And may your every day be one entirely void of addiction
Or spent in steadfast ascension of those twelve blessed steps.

Joan S.

A portion from the sales of *A Place Where Weeds and Roses Grow* goes to *Celebrate Life Recovery Service,* in support of their many programs assisting those who suffer with homelessness and addiction problems.